PARENT'S GUIDE TO COMPETITIVE GYMNASTICS

By Deborah Sevilla
Dream Believe Achieve Athletics

Intro

When my daughter entered into the world of competitive gymnastics, it was exciting, overwhelming, and very confusing. No one told me what was going on, what was normal, and what was expected at the gym, at practice, at meets. Years later as an employee of my daughter's gym, the questions I had back then are the same questions I am asked over and over by parents new to gymnastics. While working meets, I hear parents from other gyms asking the same questions.

Many gyms write and distribute their own policy handbooks to new parents. These handbooks are gym-specific, and offer helpful information regarding tuition, late fees, and practice hours, but fail to explain much of anything else. Parents wonder whether their gym's policies are the norm or unreasonable. Questions arise regarding preparation for practices and meets, parental involvement during practices, and proper etiquette at meets.

I wanted to create a guide that will help parents ease into the world of competitive gymnastics. This helpful guide was created with the help of coaches from different gyms, judges, sports **psychologists**, and fellow gym parents from around the world.

This guide is loaded with valuable information to answer your questions that are not answered in your gym's policy handbook. You will also find a glossary of gymnastics terms to help decipher "gymnast-speak", as well as forms for you to complete with your own gym's information, contacts, and other important information you need to know. All of this is easily accessible and kept together in this guide. Let's get started!

CHAPTER 1
BEFORE TEAM

Parents ask how they can get their girls on the team, how they can improve and move up faster. My advice is to first have your gymnast tell her class coach that she is interested in competing and ask what she should work on. This tells the coach that the CHILD wants it. Sometimes it is suspected that the parents want it and the child is just along for the ride. The coach should then watch a little closer and give more correction. It is always beneficial for a gymnast to practice more than once a week and most gyms give a multiclass discount. If your gymnast is missing one or two skills for team a couple of private lessons could work wonders. The most important thing is to relax, and let your gymnast enjoy class. There are many benefits to gymnastic classes.

As you may know, gymnastics promotes discipline, determination, courage, coordination and self-confidence. Children learn perseverance by falling and getting back up. Learning from mistakes builds character and self-esteem. Those who attend classes understand fairness and trust. They learn to listen, follow directions, take turns and be respectful to each other. They learn to motivate one another and to perform in front of others without anxiety. They build trusting, respectful relationships with their coaches and classmates. Setting goals will become natural and children learn to dream big. Children who are physically active are likely to make good choices when it comes to peer pressure associated with alcohol, drugs and smoking.

The coordination necessary for gymnastics also has a positive impact on cognitive abilities. Many studies show there is a strong correlation between physical fitness and academic achievement in children. Exercise encourages the brain to work at optimal capacity by causing nerve cells to multiply and strengthening their interconnections. Your child is likely to be able to focus better in school when gymnastics is a part of her life.

When your child is ready to move from recreational classes some gyms have a pre-team program. These are usually by invite / tryout only and are similar to classes but with more attention to technique and form. These groups train together 2-3 times a week usually with the same group of coaches.

Gyms find their team members in different ways. Most gyms find their team members from their classes. Some gyms hold open try-outs; an open invitation for anyone that wants to come in to try out.

CHAPTER 2
CONGRATULATIONS!

How exciting! Your child's hard work has paid off; and her talent has been recognized! Yeah! *Wait. What? More hours? More money? What's going on?* Don't panic. There is so much to learn about competitive gymnastics and no matter how long you are in the sport, there is always more to learn. Each level offers a whole new experience for both you and your gymnast.

Having a child on the gymnastics team can be a great bonding experience for a family, but it can also be a huge burden on both your time and finances. It can be a difficult decision, so it is important to know what you are getting into before you say yes.

The Decision

When my daughter was 6 years old, she had big dreams of being on the gymnastics team. At her gym, a gymnast had to be 7 years old and have a series of skills in order to be invited onto the team. With the promise of team dangled in front of her, she worked very hard on those skills. That summer when she finally got the last skill, a kip, she was on cloud nine. They told her that since she would be 7 before the first competition, she could be on the team and let her try on a warm-up jacket. Then they sat me down in the office. They started to explain the expenses, and I remember the owner looking at me and saying, "Make sure you know what you're getting yourself into before you say yes." Okay, it would have been nice if she had this conversation with me BEFORE ever mentioning the team to my star struck 6 year old. My heart just dropped and I took a deep breath. My husband had just been laid off and I knew for us there was no other choice. I had to make it work. I asked about discounts for paying in full and was offered a few hundred dollars off if I handed over the full year's tuition. I opened a new credit card and just charged the whole year. My monthly credit card payments were lower than the gym's monthly installments but the interest – ugh! Family members chipped in and purchased her uniform as her Christmas present. That year was hard, but we made it work and thankfully we got back on our feet again. Truth be told, even if they had spoken to me about it before, I would not have discouraged her, but I may have been a little better prepared. If money is an issue, have a private conversation with the gym. Do not ask for breaks or special deals; instead, ask about payment options and fundraising.

It is not easy for most of us. I know a few moms who went back to work or took on extra jobs to make it work, myself included. One of those moms loves to tell everyone how hard it was and how she had to go back to work. She loves to tell the story, because years later, after a successful gymnastics career, her daughter owns and operates a successful gym. In the end it was all worth it. I agree, because that is the gym where my daughter is now training, and her daughter is my daughter's coach.

Another thing to take into consideration is that competitive gymnastics is not for everyone. Not all kids can take the pressure of being judged, and I cannot blame them! Competition can cause anxiety, depression, anger and frustration. If they cannot find the excitement and fun in competing, they may not be cut out for it, no matter how talented they are. Notice I said "fun in competition," not "winning". No one wins all the time, and competition is not all about the win. Right about now, a few fathers just gasped and a couple of mothers swooned! By definition competition is all about the win! If you're not going to win, why compete? Hear me out. Competition can be a great experience; however, if you or your gymnast goes into it solely for "the win", you will quickly cross the crazy parent line and your child will burn out. Children like to feel proud of themselves and let's face it, parents love to brag. Please, if you choose to take the competitive step, focus on small victories and accomplishments, not scores and placements.

Working a meet, I met a very young level 4 gymnast. It was her second year competing. I found her and her mother in the bathroom before the meet. Her daughter was vomiting in the toilet. The mother looked at me very matter of fact and said, "She does this before every meet, but she loves it". She loves throwing up? *Who loves throwing up?* This is a gymnast that probably should not be competing, or maybe is not ready. I have seen many gymnasts thrive on competition day. The excitement of it all! Getting out there and doing what they love and cheering on their team. Win or lose, it is the experience that is important.

Gymnastics is not an easy sport, but with the hard work comes amazing benefits. The USAG's slogan is "Start Here, Go Anywhere". Gymnastics builds strong people by developing a strong body and mind. With the physical strength and flexibility comes socialization, discipline, respect, organization, self-motivation, work ethic and time management, to name a few. A gymnast learns how to handle setbacks and how to be a good sport; how to get back up after falling and how to conquer fears. They learn if they work hard enough, they can do what seems to be impossible.

Age

Competitive gymnasts range in age at all levels and compete against their peers. Gymnasts are divided into age divisions at every level. I can't tell you how many times I have heard a parent say, "She's already 11, isn't she too old? *Why bother?*" Why bother?! Stop for a second. If your child starts competing at age 11, is she going to the Olympics? Probably not, but is that the only reason to compete in gymnastics? I should hope not!

I once saw a 34 year old mother compete Copper (one of the lowest level) at a meet. She was achieving a lifetime dream and everyone cheered her on. She did not compete against the kids. Instead, she was in an 18 and over age division. It is about the training; it is about setting goals and achieving them; it is about the experience. She had the time of her life! I also saw a YouTube video of an older woman competing on beam and she was inspirational! So no, you are never too old to learn something new.

How young is too young? While gymnastics classes usually starts at 18 months with someone special; children cannot compete until they reach their 4th birthday for USAG level 1. That said most gyms start their competitive teams at level 2 (5years old) or 3 (6 years old). Xcel and USAIGC start at 5 years old. Additionally, each gym has its own standards. For example, even though USAIGC requires a gymnast to be 6 years old to compete bronze; the gym wouldn't allow my daughter to compete until she was 7.

Expenses

Competition leotards can cost anywhere from $75 to $200 EACH. Most teams have custom designed leotards and yes, you must buy the same one; no, you do not get a say in the design. All teams compete in matching uniforms chosen by the gym. Ask your gym about used leotards. Your daughter may be the same size another gymnast just outgrew. Leotards stay in good shape for a long time. Some people will tell you competition leotards or even all leotards should be hand washed and laid flat to dry. I do not know about you, but I do not have that kind of time on my hands. I machine wash in cold water and toss them over the railing to dry. Trust me when I say – no matter what the tag says – do not put leotards or warm-ups in the dryer! I have lost a few when they were tossed in the dryer by accident. If the dryer runs to hot your leos will have those lovely dryer circles burned in to them.

Leotards, especially competition leotards, should fit like a bathing suit. That means very little growing room. Nothing looks worse than a baggy leotard, except maybe undies sticking out of the bottom! More about that later. Warm-up suit costs start around $75 and go up from there. When it comes to warm-ups, you can allow some growing room. Sleeves can be rolled up a little and pants rolled up at the waist or pinned at the bottom. Again, ask about the availability of used warm-ups. A little heads-up: as soon as your gymnast gets their warm-up, they are going to immediately try to wear part of it to school. They are excited, and who can blame them? Try to avoid this if you can as accidents happen; imagine if your gymnast returned home from school with grass stains on the back of those custom order warm-up pants. Compromise by buying a team sweatshirt, if available

Tuition does not cover everything. There are fees; meet fees, coach's fees, travel expenses, and membership fees. When it comes to fees: every gym is different. There are a few parents who look up the "cost" of a meet and get upset that they are being asked to pay more than the entry fee posted. There are a couple of things to take into consideration regarding the breakdown of meet fees. There are individual entry fees that the gym has to pay to enter each gymnast and there is a team entry fee which is usually split among the members of the team. I hate that I have to say it, but it is not optional and you cannot opt out of the team event. Please remember that gymnastics is a team sport and the team experience can be the best part. Coach's fees are not always itemized. The team shares in the cost of the coach(es) coming to the meet and working. Would *you* work all day or weekend for free? If there is travel involved, coaches need to be compensated for plane fare, hotel and other travel expenses. Remember this is their job.

Fundraising / Booster Clubs / Parent Associations

If your gym offers any fundraising, this is a great opportunity not only to raise money for your gymnast/team, but to get to know the other parents. Every gym operates differently and the involvement allowed and expected from parents and gymnasts vary. There are gyms on both ends of the spectrum, some gyms require a certain number of hours and involvement; others want you to drop off your gymnast and leave it all to them.

Booster Club fees are similar to PTA dues. Not all gyms have booster clubs and membership is usually not optional. Booster clubs are beneficial, helping families with expenses and running fundraising events. If there is a booster club at your gym, make sure you find out your obligations. For example, you may be required to work a meet session or participate in a fundraiser. Parent Associations work differently and membership is usually optional. They also help organize fundraisers.

Welcome to the team

So, you decided to take the plunge! At one time or another you will regret it, but do not worry, the feeling will pass.

Every gym operates differently, but there are several universal truths or guidelines. This book should help you get going and not feel too lost. In the back of the book there are questionnaires and worksheets to help you gather all the information you need. Ask if your gym has a policy handbook, then READ it cover to cover and keep it in a safe place for reference.

CHAPTER 3
TEAM PRACTICE

Practice

If gymnastics was easy, it would be called football. The move from recreational gymnastics to competitive gymnastics can be a difficult transition because of the increase in conditioning and correction. Doing a skill is no longer good enough; now they are being asked to point toes and straighten knees. This can be hard for a gymnast to take and can suck the fun out of gymnastics. Hang in there. Let the coaches do their job. Be patient and let your gymnast adjust. Perseverance is a great quality. The fun should return.

It is important to arrive on time for practice. That is when the gymnasts stretch and warm-up. It is very important, at every level that gymnasts warm up correctly. Team gymnasts' warm-up is much more involved than the recreational classes. Once your gymnast has been doing this for a few years they can warm themselves up; until then they need direction. Do not be surprised if your gymnast comes home complaining that it is "too hard" or complains about sore muscles. Eventually she will adapt to the new regimen. Conditioning is very important and very difficult. Some parents compare conditioning to military boot camp. Gymnastics is a very demanding sport and requires a person to have total control over their body, and that requires strength.

Attire

Most gymnasts have anywhere between 10-40 leotards in their dresser. In my opinion, your gymnast will need at least enough to make 1-2 weeks of practice without you having to do laundry. For example, if your gymnast is in the gym 2 days a week, it is a good idea to have 2-4 leotards. There is nothing worse than realizing there are no clean leotards minutes before practice. Let's be honest . . . we all fall behind on the laundry from time to time; however, leotards are not cheap. To reduce costs, take a look on eBay. If you can find someone selling a "lot" in your size, or a size up, you can get some great deals. Some gyms have leo rummage sales as fundraisers or exchange systems in place to recycle leotards from the older to the little kids. Leotards will last if taken care of. Our gym has a leo fundraiser a few times a year and some of the leotards are on their 4th or 5th owners! The kids look forward to cleaning out their closets and the little ones love wearing the older girls' stuff. Parents absolutely LOVE getting some money for their outgrown leos as well as the opportunity to get their hands on new ones at a great price. If you are not thrilled with the idea of a new-to-you leotard, check out manufacturers' websites for clearance deals.

A word about shorts: many gyms do not allow team gymnasts to wear shorts over their leotards, and I am not aware of any that will let them wear t-shirts. The coach needs to see the line of the body to accurately spot and correct. Some gyms allow "bar shorts", which are really tight shorts. Respect your gym's dress code. Team members set the example and represent the gym. I understand that maturing girls may feel insecure and want to cover up. Remember they will not be permitted to wear anything other than their leotard in competition. They need to get used to it and get comfortable.

It is very common for gyms to have viewing policies for team parents. Respect their policy. There are many reasons for policies, but the one universal truth is that parents are a distraction. Come on, you know it is true. Coaches do not want kids (and they do it at all ages) looking to their parents for approval. They need to focus and not worry about whether you are watching. If you need to get a message to your gymnast during practice, please talk to the office staff and they will relay the message. Do not try to get their attention out on the gym floor.

If you have a question about the way your daughter's coach is teaching or if you have an issue about something that is happening during workouts, you should bring it to the attention of your daughter's coach. You might find that what you believe is a negative situation is a simple misunderstanding. Chapter 8 will discuss dealing with problems in more detail. It is important to remember that the relationship between coach and gymnast is a strong bond, requiring the gymnast to fully trust that the coach knows what they are doing and has them if they fall. You need to trust that your child's coach knows what they are doing. If you question the coach, it creates doubt in your gymnast.

Practice time

Competitive gymnasts spend much more time in the gym than recreational gymnasts. As they move up in level, that time increases and varies by gym. The following are guidelines and averages by level and does not take the age of the gymnast into account. You know your child and what she can handle. Is homework getting done and are her grades good? Is she exhausted after practice and/or does she have trouble getting up in the morning? Is she cranky and/or overtired?

USAG		
	Level 3	6 hours (3 days x 2 hours)
According to a survey of US gyms by GymnasticsZone.com	Level 4	8.75 hours
	Level 5	11 hours
	Level 6	13.5 hours
	Level 7	15 hours(5 days x 3 hours)
	Level 8	16.5 hours
	Level 9	18 hours (6 days x 3 hours)
USAIGC	Copper	3-4 hours
(USAIGC 2013-2015 Rules & Policies)	Bronze	6 hours
	Silver	6-8 hours
	Gold	8-10 hours
	Platinum	12-15 hours
	Premier	up to 16 hours

What about homework?

Gymnasts have an amazing sense of discipline and time management. I have always told my daughter that she was not going to the gym until she completed her homework. Having that mindset, she learned early on how to manage her time. My daughter can complete her homework neatly and correctly while eating dinner before it is time to leave for the gym. I know other girls that have mastered the art of doing homework and eating dinner in the car on the way to the gym. I have seen the older girls lend a hand to the younger with studying and homework while stretching. The best is when a gymnast is reading a classic book and the coaches get in on the discussion! My older daughter would have never passed 9th grade English without the coach's help and discussions. These are my experiences at my gym that has a big family feel. I wish it was the same everywhere, but I know it is not. At some gyms it is 100% gymnastics and no time for anything else. Find *your* balance.

Homeschooling?

Some gyms encourage homeschooling as part of their program. These gymnasts are usually in the gym for a morning workout, complete school work, and then have an afternoon workout. I can see how this is beneficial. In addition to an increase in hours, most gyms have very few classes during the day, freeing up coaches and equipment for team members. Only you know if this is something that is right for you. Is your child going to miss out on important social interactions? Is it something your child wants? If I asked my daughter if she wanted to be homeschooled and go to the gym in the morning, she would answer with a resounding yes; however, if she thought I was serious in my offer, I do not think she would give up her school friends quite so fast. I do believe it is important to have more than one group of friends. Nothing is more devastating to a child than a falling out with their "group". They can very quickly feel alone and isolated. That is the one thing I always liked about gymnastics for my daughter. If there are problems in her school group she always has her gym friends and vice versa. I have heard of public and private schools arranging school schedules to enable athletes to have both the morning workout and a school experience.

Shawn Johnson, 2008 Olympic balance beam gold medalist and team all-around and floor exercise silver medalist, attended public high school and maintained a balanced lifestyle. She was on the honor roll and attended social events such as football games and dances. In spring of 2009, she left public school and got a private tutor so she could participate in the opportunities provided to her through the Olympics.

Eat, Sleep, Gymnastics

My daughter has a sweatshirt that says "I Can't, I have Practice". Older gymnasts joke about "not having a life". Truth be told, gymnastics is their life. How many of us have gymnasts that freak out if the gym closes for snow day or a holiday? They would rather be there. Gymnastics relies heavily on repetition and muscle memory. Some gyms have you sign a contact, and they take it seriously. You do not miss practice – ever. They say its commitment and dedication. Let's take a minute. No vacations, no birthday parties. As a family, you have to find a balance. You can be committed and dedicated without sacrificing everything. Do you have to sacrifice family vacations and those memories and experiences? With the crazy gym contract aside – most coaches do not have a problem with missing a day or two for family vacations, special occasions, or even a mental health day. If you went to work as often as your child goes to the gym, wouldn't you need the occasional day off? Keep in mind, if your gymnast is missing days regularly you can't take it out on the coach if she does not perform as well as her teammates that are putting in the time.

Over the years my daughter's friends have learned her schedule and what days she has off from the gym and they plan to get together accordingly. As gymnasts get older, it is not just social temptations, but the school obligations; orchestra concerts, school trips, extra help, etc.

Something to consider is tying family mini vacations into away meets. When you have a competition where a hotel stay is needed, find out the area's local attractions. Your gymnast will not be competing 24 hours of each day. There are many interesting little places around the United States and some great family memories can be made without missing gym time or breaking the bank. In a few weeks we are traveling to Syracuse, NY for a competition. We happened to find a mountain roller coaster open year round in the area. It is not a trip to the Bahamas but it is a little family fun!

If, heaven forbid, your child could no longer do gymnastics, what would she do with her time? Who would she hang out with? Many gymnasts express feeling lost without gymnastics and their teammates. What's that saying about having all your eggs in one basket? Having friends and interests outside of gymnastics is healthy and strongly encouraged.

Carpool 101

A few parents have a "Gym Taxi" decal on their car. My husband used to refer to the car as the "gym bus" some nights when it is packed with 5 kids. Driving back and forth to the gym can seem like an endless chore, particularly if you live far from the gym. To save time, gas and stress try setting up a carpool system with a few parents from your gymnast's team. A successful carpool is dependable, on time and benefits all parties.

The first task is to find other carpool participants. Start talking, strike up conversations with other parents. See who lives in or around your neighborhood. Ask them if they'd be interested in working out a carpool schedule. Talk to your gymnast, she may know who lives where. Make sure you are aware if some parents' nannies or older siblings are doing their share of the carpooling you will likely want to gain additional information, including their driving experience. You should have their number, and they should have yours in case of emergencies.

Organize a schedule with all interested families, determining what days and times work best for each. Make sure responsibilities are distributed evenly, that everyone has the schedule and each other's contact information

Getting into an existing carpool can be difficult. First you need to determine is the car is full and if you would be on or out of the way. How can you contribute? Do not be offended if the answer is no. One more stop may just feel like too much or take too much time. There was one girl that would need a ride home every now and then. Even though technically it was "on our way" it was 20 minute detour from our usual route. On a school night those 20 minutes made big difference.

Carpool Etiquette

Set guidelines. Every family has different car rules. You may allow eating in the car and others do not. Some parents aren't opposed to kids sharing seatbelts, squeezing an extra kid in. Do you have a loud car with a lot of talking and singing, or do you need quiet? Make sure the kids and other parents are all aware of the car rules.

Kids participating in the carpool should be ready on time and parents should be home for the drop off. If the driver is running late he or she should try to let everyone know.

If it is your day to drive and you cannot make it be sure to inform everyone in the carpool as soon as possible. Do not leave people hanging at the last minute. Have a back-up plan. Kids get sick, parents get sick, cars break down and there should be a backup plan. For example, the backup for pickups on Mondays is Chrissy, who needs to get a phone call by 2pm if she's needed to drive the car pool.

CHAPTER 4
MEET BASICS

The meet takes how long? The average meet can take as little as three and a half hours or as long as six hours, depending on the number of gymnasts and how many levels are in the session.

> TIP Check the start time of the session after yours; you should be out before the next session, or close to it. The exception is when a meet overlaps sessions by having warm-up, competition, and/or awards in separate areas.

Warm-up time is the time the gymnasts are expected to start warming up. It is very rare for anyone to be allowed in before this time. I have spent many hours out in the cold, rain, and/or snow waiting to get into a meet because the session before is running late or I was running early! No one, especially the people running the meet, want to run late. If this happens, take it easy on them; trust me, they are more stressed about it than you are. The meet time or competition time is usually 30 minutes after the warm-up time and is when the competition is expected to begin.

After warm-up, all the gymnasts line up and march in to the gym to be presented to the audience and judges. The national anthem is played. Note: to save time, some meets will have the gymnasts at their first event for the playing of the anthem. When my gymnast was young, I loved the march in. It was a great photo-op. Now that she is older, I have a "let's get on with it" attitude.

The gymnasts now warm-up on the events and compete. Events are competed in Olympic order. Olympic order is vault, bars, beam, and then floor.   If your child starts on floor, her next event is vault, then bars. Occasionally a team might rotate out of order if an event is backed up; for example, floor has a lot of teams waiting, but no one is vaulting. This is rare and only happens when there are a lot of kids and the meet is in danger of running late. Gymnasts receive scores from the judges on each event on cards. Your coach gets these cards at the end of the meet and gives them out at awards or at the gym after the conclusion of the meet.

After all gymnasts have competed in your session, there is an award ceremony. Usually the gym needs 15-30 minutes to compile all the scores. During this time, some meets will hold handstand contests. If an alternate space is available, many gyms will hold awards in another room. This enables the host gym to get the next session in and going. You should always stay for awards! This is considered good sportsmanship. True story: I once waited over an hour for awards where my daughter and her teammates received nothing – I mean nothing! They sat together eating snacks and cheering on the other teams saying things like, "Oh yeah, I saw her bar routine; it was amazing." They knew they were not coming home with anything, but not one of them was interested in leaving. I was very proud of each and every one of them.

More than you need to know

USA Gymnastics has 4 competition formats: Traditional, Modified Traditional, Capital Cup (Non-Traditional) and Modified Capital Cup (Modified Non-Traditional). In Traditional Formats warm-up occurs on all 4 events before competition begins. Modified Traditional applies when there is only one set of equipment. In the Capital Cup formats, the gymnasts warm-up on an event and then compete on that event immediately afterwards. Modified Capital format applies when there is more than one set of equipment in the competition gym. Capital Cup is the most popular meet format in use.

Meet Times

Meets are generally scheduled on Saturday and Sunday with check in times as early as 7:45 a.m. and competition ending as late as 10 p.m. Yes, that is a long day for volunteers, meet workers, judges and coaches. Keep that in mind! With the increasing numbers of gymnasts, more meets now have Friday sessions so that all gymnasts can have the opportunity to compete. This is especially true the closer the meet is to states, as there are gymnasts still trying to qualify. A meet can be scheduled during school hours. While gyms try very hard to avoid this and respect a parent's decision to scratch (drop out) because of school, they will not refund meet fees after the scratch date for this or any other reason. The number of competitors determines the meet times and sessions so they have to limit the number of competitors they will accept. Usually there are 3 to 4 sessions per day in a club hosted meet. It is possible to have as many as 12 to 16 sessions in a day if they overlap in large venues. As all meets run on a strict schedule, it is very important that gymnasts arrive on time and ready to compete for their session to ensure that everyone has an enjoyable experience. A competition will not wait for a gymnast to arrive.

Note: you may not be able to enter the gym before the stretch time. If you are the first session, they may be still setting up concessions and spectator areas. If you are not the first session, most gyms cannot safely admit a session until the previous session is completed and leaves. People working the meet are mostly volunteers from the host gym. They are gym parents, just like you, so please try to be courteous. Often the gymnasts will enter the gym before the spectators.

Meet Schedules

Make sure you get a meet schedule from your gym! These schedules are tentative and subject to change. The majority of gyms hand out a schedule that includes the name of the meet, location, host gym name and any other information needed. You will notice right away the dates on the schedule include the whole weekend. Thankfully, your child is not competing the entire weekend. This is because no one knows which session, day and time your gymnast's level/age will compete until approximately *one to two weeks prior to the meet.* You are given the entire weekend to block off to avoid conflicts. Do not call a host gym for meet information. Trust that your gym will provide the information needed as soon as they are able. Be aware that meet schedules are always tentative and can change even a day before the meet.

It is important to note some meets close out fast. Your gym has to reserve and pay for your spot months in advance. The scratch date is the last day your gym can pull you out of a competition and receive a refund. If you scratch after that date, most gyms require you to pay the meet fee because they cannot receive a refund. I know you are thinking "what about injuries and illnesses?" You couldn't possibly know that in advance. Unfortunately, a scratch for any reason after the scratch date is not refundable. Do NOT, under any circumstances call a host gym and scratch your gymnasts or try to get a refund. They cannot help you.

Venues

Meets are held in one of two locations: A club meet is held at the host club's gym, and an arena meet is held at a nearby high school, college gym or public arena. In a club, seating is unpredictable. Spectators are often squeezed around the perimeter of the competitive area, sitting on folding metal chairs or on small bleachers. Parents usually prefer the arena meets because of their spaciousness and bleacher seating; however, an arena meet will charge more for admission, sometimes as much as 2-3 times what a club meet would cost. The gymnast entry fees are also usually much higher at these venues to offset the high cost.

Admission

Yes, there are admission fees! All meets charge an admission fee for each session and may offer a discount for full day passes or a family rate.   Admission information is usually posted on the host club's website prior to the meet. Many parents are surprised by this but fail to realize the expense of holding a meet. Even at a club meet, the gym has to purchase the awards, pay staff, rent seating, and pay judges. On top of that the USAG/USAIGC collects an established amount per competing athlete. Do not forget: a gym has to cancel classes to host a meet as well. Hosting a meet takes months of preparation and is a lot of work. Let's be honest; if the gym did not profit even a little, most gyms would not host a meet.

Concessions

There are usually snacks, candy, soda, water and the ever-important coffee. Do not expect actual food at all meets, but many will have hot pretzels, hot dogs, and bagels. If you have never been to a venue before and it is lunch time, plan to grab something ahead of time. I once went to a meet and there was nothing available for sale, not even a vending machine or water fountain was available. One of the parents ran out to a convenience store to grab everyone chips. It is rare, but it happens.

T-shirts and sweatshirts are sometimes available with the meet name. The smaller sized t-shirts sell out early; so you may not want to wait until the end to make your purchase. Many gymnasts like to get a t-shirt at each meet to wear to school the next day, especially the young gymnasts. Warning - This can become an expensive habit! Headbands, pins, jewelry, leotards and bags are also seen at larger meets.

Programs are sometimes available at large meets and range from free to $20. These programs generally have the names of the gym and/or competitors inside, as well as an area to track scores. They often sell ad space to companies and individuals can purchase a space to wish their gymnast luck or to send a special message. Information is generally available on the host gym's website and purchase deadlines vary, but are usually a month in advance. Program sales are often a fundraiser for the gym or charity. Should you buy one? I know moms that buy one every time so they can see who is competing and then keep it as a souvenir. Personally, I only buy one if the proceeds are for a charity or if it is a big state or national meet. For example, my daughter attends a Flip for a Cure meet that benefits breast cancer every year. That program I buy. Honestly, one thing I do not need is more paper in my house!

Parking

Parking is usually free at Club Meets but is cramped since the facilities are not designed for large attendance numbers, so plan to arrive early to find a place to park or have time to walk to the entrance. It is not uncommon for a host gym to arrange parking down the road or across the street. Carpooling is often recommended. Arena meets usually have plenty of parking but may charge anywhere from $5 to $30.

Changing facilities

Changing facilities are usually not available or readily found, so it is always best for your athlete to arrive at the meet site in their uniform, ready to compete, if only to reduce the frustration of trying to find a place to change or the panic that comes when one realizes that they left part of their uniform at home. There are often long lines before a meet for the bathroom because girls are in the stalls changing.

Equipment

The host gym or an equipment supplier supplies all equipment at the meet and it has to meet USAG/USAIGC standards to be a sanctioned meet.

Siblings

Meets are not the most exciting event for siblings, especially younger ones. Plan to bring quiet activities that will keep them seated and occupied (at times in a very limited space) for 3.5 to 5 hours as there will likely be no safe place for them to roam or run, nor should they! Please do not leave siblings unattended in hallways or concession areas. Not only are you wasting your money paying for them to get in and the constant snacks they are going to want, but the people working the meet are not babysitters.   During one session at my gym, there were 6 kids running around playing tag! I constantly stopped what I was doing and checked on them because their parents were not watching them. DVD players, computers, and games on phones or hand held devices without earphones are distracting and disturbing to the people around you. The sound may also pick up when others attempt to record their child's routine. Remember that viewing can be poor, the floor is usually dirty from traffic and chalk, bathrooms often have lines, and in order to get pictures/video of your athlete, you may need to move around. There is usually no room for strollers or carriages, especially at club meets. *Please consider hiring a babysitter if you have young children.*

Meet hotels

Host clubs usually block off rooms in local hotels that meet most families' expectations for satisfactory lodging, have a very competitive group rate, and are close to the meet site. Staying in the same hotel as your team can be a big part of the team experience and a lot of fun. Some gyms and teams have a tradition of decorating each other's hotel room doors. My daughter's team decorates each other's doors with homemade signs, photos and streamers.

Cameras and video cameras

Flash photography and lights on video cameras are not allowed at any meet because of the risk of temporarily blinding a gymnast while they are performing, causing injury. There are NO exceptions to this rule. Ever. Check your cameras and video recorders prior to recording and taking photos. Some cameras have what is called a focus light. Your flash might be off, but the camera still shines a light to help it focus. This is not allowed. My husband always takes one photo of the floor at the start of a meet to ensure no light will shine out onto the competition area. I also must mention that you may not use a flash even if you are taking a photo in the spectator area. It is surprising how far a flash can travel and be seen from the other side of the gym. You may be able to move around the spectator area but will NEVER be allowed to enter the competitive floor. Please do not ask to go onto the competitive floor at any time or try to sneak on. Personally, I tend to find a spot in the back against the wall and take turns with my fellow team moms standing on a chair to video. People fight for those front row seats, but they are often not the best seats in the house. Try to get up high. There is always a chance a coach, gymnast or entire team will suddenly appear in front of you. If this happens, I know it is hard, but remember, you are all there for one purpose: for the gymnasts to compete, not for you to get a picture or video. You will need a zoom lens on your equipment for most photography. Have extra batteries for your cameras because electrical outlets are usually unavailable. I wish I had photos of all the parents I have seen crawling under bleachers trying to plug in their camera!

If you have a point and shoot camera or your cell phone, you will most likely not be able to capture action shots inside the gym. Even with an expensive digital SLR, getting the shot can be challenging and frustrating. Bottom line: to capture action, you need at least a 640 shutter speed with a high ISO. Remember, no flash. A good bench line for a lens is f2.8.

Photographers

ALL HAIL THE PROFESSIONAL PHOTOGRAPHER! If there is a professional photographer at the meet, check it out. This is a great way to get action pictures of your gymnast. Due to lighting and venue limitations, they are usually able to get those perfect shots that parents are rarely positioned to get for themselves. Many offer packages and require a deposit to take the photographs. After the meet, they post all the photos they take, usually around 200-300 photos, to a website where you get to review, choose and order. Even though my husband takes amazing photographs, I still try to do this once a year. I do not get a big collage, but I like getting the digital files and/or a couple of prints, depending on the deal.

CHAPTER 5
COMPETITION TIME

Getting Ready

A quick note about underwear: most gymnasts go commando, which is without underwear under their leotard. If that grosses you or your gymnast out, invest in underwear specifically made to be worn under a leotard. Most leotard companies (GK, Snowflake etc.) make underwear designed to wear under leotards. In my honest opinion, there is nothing more distracting at a competition than bloomers hanging out of the bottom of the leotard or seeing stripes through the leotard. While we are talking about unmentionables, older gymnasts need to be aware of their bra choice. We had a gymnast show up for a meet not realizing that you could see the leopard print bra through the leotard! At this point, there is very little you can do besides hope the judges do not notice, and if they do they laugh and not deduct!

When you are getting your daughter ready for a meet, make sure that you do her hair in a way that is approved by your gym and that will stay intact for the entire meet.   Some teams have a standard hairstyle and/or barrette that all gymnasts wear.   Many girls like to use a little hair spray glitter. Be sure to ask your gym if this is permitted. Some gyms are very particular with the presentation of their girls and are trying to uphold a certain image. Remember, a meet is not a dance recital, make-up is not needed, fancy hair clips tend to fall out, and jewelry is not permitted. Also, make sure that all nail polish (fingers and toes) is removed before your daughter competes. She can get a deduction for having polished nails and toes.

Is the uniform clean and ready? It has happened to the best of gym moms. Picture it: 6am the morning and the meet is at 8 a.m. the leotard or warm-up is not where it should be, or it is dirty, or suddenly does not fit!

Avoid waiting until the day of the meet to check that everything is ready. Pack the gym bag the day or night before. Make sure grips, braces, tape, and anything else needed is in the bag.

> TIP: Before your first meet, it is a great idea to have a test run by sending her to practice in the hair style. After practice, see if it is still neat and make sure it was not in the way. For example, pony tails or buns put in the wrong place can be distracting or in the way for a back extension roll, hair hanging too long down the back can swing forward into your gymnast's eyes, a tight french braid could give your gymnast a headache…you never know until you try.

In the bag

Remember you will most likely not be in contact with your gymnast until after the competition is over, so pack for her anything you think she might need. Here are some suggestions:

Gymnast Bag

- Music: if your gymnast has her own music, always have a CD in her bag – just in case
- Deodorant
- Hair supplies depending on the style (bobby pins, barrettes, and hairspray)
- Band-Aids
- Healthy snack: Send a snack that does not stain or create crumbs. Also try to refrain from sending nuts of any kind. There are many children with life-threatening nut allergies and it is very easy to contaminate equipment
- Water / sports drinks. Avoid drinks with sugar or carbonation.
- Athletic Tape & Under Wrap
- Grips / Wrist Guards (if used)
- Flip flops or slippers for trips to the bathroom. Some coaches have the gymnast leave their coat and shoes with parents. You don't want your gymnast going into public bathrooms barefoot.
- Medical supplies (if used often) For example: Inhaler, Benadryl, Aspirin, Contact solution (if needed)

Parents, you will need some things too!

- Cash to get into the meet and for snacks or drinks. Some meets do not accept credit cards.
- Camera! Just turn off that flash!
- Video Camera
- Stadium seat or pillow if you have a sensitive tush
- Pencil or pen to take down scores
- Scorebook / paper

Chapter 6
AT THE MEET!

Say Goodbye and wish them luck!

At gymnastics meets, parents are prohibited from being on the competitive floor because of competitive sanction rules and safety certification policies. The only adults allowed in the competitive area are judges, those helping run the competition, and coaches. Remember, USAG coaches are safety certified and should be trained to handle injuries. If your daughter starts crying, allow the coach to handle the situation. I know how hard it is to watch your child cry, but it is important for them to learn how to deal with setbacks during competition without parental help. Trust your coaches to calm your daughter. If you are needed on the floor, your coach will signal for you. After the meet/awards is over, they will come and see you.

Meet Etiquette

Please do not coach your gymnast at meets (or at the gym). This is the coaches' job. Do not contact or talk to your gymnast or the coaches once they are on the competitive floor. They need to focus all their energy on the competition with as few distractions as possible. Cheer for all members of your team, and feel free to cheer for fine performances turned in by the gymnasts of other teams, but be respectful. Over cheering can distract gymnasts and annoy judges, and no one wants to annoy the judges! Never heckle other teams or speak badly about other children. You never know who is sitting around you, and there is also a very good chance you will see these parents from other gyms at future meets.

As you watch your gymnast try to focus on improvement in skills, and do not compare scores to other gymnasts. No matter how hard we try, and all parents try we do not understand scoring. There is always someone that fell on beam and scored higher than someone that did not fall, or a similar occurrence. Again, you have to trust in your coach. If something seems off they will handle it. Do not, under any circumstances, approach a judge. Just like the other parents, you will see these judges again at other meets and you do not want them to remember you, your child, or your gym in an unfavorable light!

When moving around in the spectator area, please look around you first! There are other parents videotaping or trying to photograph. Routines are so short. You could unintentionally block someone's view of an entire vault or bar routine! If you take a front row seat, do not stand up to take a video your child. Remember, there are usually 4 events going on at the same time and a lot of people sitting behind you.

I wish this did not need to be said, but be courteous to the host gym. Try to clean up after yourself. For example, do not leave a full cup of coffee under your chair, or toss your garbage on the floor.

What's Going On?

A meet can be very confusing. Every gymnast gets to warm-up on each event. Before the gymnast competes the judge will salute the gymnast that they are ready to score and the gymnast salutes the judge that they are ready to begin. This is how you will know the difference between warm-up and competition. The gymnast will salute again to mark the completion of the routine. Each team and gymnast gets a certain amount of time to warm-up on each event. Special note about the beam: On beam the gymnasts often get a timed warm-up on one beam and then a quick "touch" on the competition beam. Touches are usually between competitors while the judges are calculating scores. Again, watch for your gymnast to salute.

Here is where there is a lot of confusion. If the meet has scores manually flashed after each event, the score flashed immediately following the gymnast is NOT their score. Think about it: the judges can't calculate the score that fast. That score is for the gymnast before them. Some gyms have invested in digital scoring. At these gyms, there are monitors or screens on display. The gymnast's name, event, and score will appear on the screen. Scores are only flashed once. What if you missed it? Please do not bother anyone working the meet. Generally speaking, they are really busy and do not readily have the information. Do not try to get the attention of your gymnast or your coach; they are also busy. If no other parent from your team caught it, your coaches can give it to you afterward. Additionally, most gyms will post the score on their website within a week following the meet.

Team Line-Ups

Many parents wonder how the order the gymnasts compete in is determined. It is an incorrect assumption that the order is always from worse to best gymnast. At some meets, such as state championships, the order is predetermined and the coaches have no control over the line-up. When the coaches do arrange the line-ups, many times the gymnasts are lined up in the order of equipment settings. For example; for vault, the coach will line up the gymnasts according to vault height so that the vault table does not have to be adjusted and readjusted several times. Bar settings are also taken into consideration. If it is a large team, the order established by these settings will hold true for all the other events as it can difficult to change the order at each event. I recently discovered my daughter always goes last on floor, if the coaches are given the option, because she is asthmatic and they want to give her time to rest. Other gymnasts may go first because of their nerves. If you have a question or concern about the order, ask your coach at the gym, not at the meet. Their explanation may surprise you.

Scoring

Scoring at gymnastics competitions is the hardest thing to figure out. Honestly, you are better off not trying to figure it out. It could turn you into a crazy gym parent, and no one wants to be a crazy gym parent. It is better to focus on your gymnast's performance and any improvements. There are score books designed to help gymnasts with goals and achievements, such as The Dream Believe Achieve score books and journals. Here are some pointers to remember. All judges are different. This is a very subjective sport. Your gymnast's scores from meet to meet can vary greatly, even if the routine they perform is similar. It is very hard to compare scores from meet to meet since it can vary on how hard or easy the judge is, the level of other competitors and sometimes for no reason at all.

Compulsory Gymnasts' (USAG Levels 3-5) routines all have a start value of 10.0. Optional Gymnasts' (USAIGC Copper, Bronze, Silver, Gold, Platinum and Premier & USAG Levels 6 & over) routines have different start values. This start value depends on what skills are in your gymnast's routine. Each level has different requirements that the gymnasts must fulfill in order to get the maximum start value. Higher levels can receive bonus points.

Once the gymnast starts her routine, judges take deductions from the gymnast start value. Examples of items that the judges can deduct for: falling, stopping (if it is not supposed to be in the routine), bent arms, bent legs, flex feet, omitting a skill, receiving a spot, not enough height, wrong body angles, and so much more. If you have any questions on what your gymnast needs to improve to increase her scores, talk to her coach *at the gym*.

In Elite level gymnastics, the gymnasts receive two scores: an execution score and a difficulty score. The execution score starts at a maximum of ten points, with execution errors subtracted during the routine. The difficulty score is the degree of difficulty contained in the routine. The Elite gymnast's final score is the total of the difficulty and execution scores, less any deductions for neutral errors. Neutral errors include those for stepping out of bounds or violating time requirements, as well as attire or podium violations.

Awards

Gymnasts are expected to attend the entire awards ceremony and sit with their teammates. The awards ceremony for each session is usually held about 20 to 30 minutes after the completion of the competition. Note: if sessions overlap, the coach may not be able to stay for awards because they are needed at the next level's competition. Each meet is different, and the awards given, places awarded, and age groups all vary. The host gym usually decides how many places will be awarded. While some gyms will acknowledge the top 40-50 percent in each event, others will only present awards to the top three in each event. There are also some gyms that will give out participation awards going out 100% in All Around. Participation awards are more common at lower/younger levels. The awards themselves range from ribbons to trophies, but are usually medals.

> *TIP – Label medals and trophies with the year, level, meet, event, place and score. It is nice to be able to look back and remember what each medal was for. You also may want to invest in a medal rack or hooks to display awards on your gymnast's bedroom wall.*

Age groups

Before the meet, your gym usually receives a list of gymnasts and their birthdays for confirmation. Each meet is run differently. The age of the gymnast at the time of the meet is not always the age used for groups. Sometimes it is based on the age the gymnast will be at the state championship or it is based on their age on first of the year. Many meets will evenly split the session in two or three age groups. In these cases gymnasts of the same age can end up in two different age groups.

It is not fair or at least it does not feel that way. In one age division, it is possible for 1st place to have a score of 8.5; at the same meet and same level but in different age group, a gymnast with a 9.3 may not even place! Remember, competitors are competing against their peers.

Team awards

Team scores are based on the top gymnast scores of a team per event. The number of scores taken varies by competition, but it is usually the top 3-5 scores. Teams are awarded a team trophy, plaque or banner to be displayed at the winners' home gym.

The gymnasts are dismissed after the awards have been presented and are free to return to you and leave at that time. Some team parents have traditions after meets such as going for ice cream or dinner together as a team. This tends to be especially true if the team places.

Home Gym Advantage

Parents sometimes wonder if the host gym has the upper hand. Simply put, yes and no. Yes, the hosting gymnasts are familiar with and comfortable with the equipment; however, this could also be a disadvantage if the gymnasts feel too comfortable and relaxed, which can lead to stupid mistakes. Aside from that, there are no other advantages. To keep it fair, there are rules in place to prevent judges from being affiliated with the gyms competing at meets where they are judging.

Judges

In gymnastics there are judges, not referees. Judging, by definition is to form an opinion or estimation of after careful consideration. Every judge is different, and it is important to remember they are only human. One judge may be a stickler on sickle feet, where another does not even notice it. Judges are watching for hundreds of things at a time and it is reasonable for them to have different perspectives and scores. If your gymnast, who usually scores 9s on bars, has a great routine and gets in the 8s, talk to your coach *at the gym after the meet*. If something seems off, trust that your coach will question it. Maybe bars scored low all weekend, or maybe that judge watches for something your gymnast does or does not do. This is why I stress not to get hung up on scores. If you make it all about the scores, you are liable to go crazy. Please try to enjoy the experience, and your child will do the same.

Many judges have full time weekday jobs and spend their weekends judging because of their love of their sport and the athletes. Take a moment and think about it. You sit and watch your child and by the end of the session you are ready to GO! These judges watch gymnast after gymnast for hours with only limited breaks in between. It is not an easy job. Be respectful of what they do. It is never acceptable or appropriate to approach a judge to ask about scores or any other technical aspects of the meet.

What makes them so qualified? There is a misconception that anyone can be a judge, and anyone can be a judge after completing the required classes and passing the exams! Judges have to take seminars, classes, workshops, and exams to keep their certifications every year for each level.

Chapter 7
Know Your Place

Your role

As a parent you put in a lot of time, energy and money for your child to have an opportunity to pursue their interests and dreams. This is not a business relationship where you are investing in your child and expect a return, performance wise, but because you want them to be successful and happy. You are paying a coach to coach your gymnast, let them do their job. It can be difficult to step back but when you drop your child off they are now the coach's responsibility. Hopefully you are at a gym where the coaches and gymnasts feel like second family, the gym a second home. It is not your job to correct or motivate your gymnast. It is your job to support your gymnast on their gymnastics roller coaster ride full of ups and downs. Be there to listen to and support, not to judge, and not to nag. After a bad day at the gym, which *everyone* has, the last thing a gymnast needs is to get in the car and get drilled on their performance. You are their solitude and as their parent are there for support.

There is a fine line between 'supportive gym parent' and 'crazy gym parent'. Of course, many parents want to be involved with their kids' activities so that they can be assured they're guided in a safe and nurturing direction. As 'supportive gym parents' we are the ones getting them up early in the morning, driving them to practice and paying the bills. All of those things are necessary for the child to be able to participate in the sport, unfortunately, we also have seen those parents that cross over into the "obsessive/overbearing parent" (aka 'crazy gym parent').

There is also a thin line between proud and crazy gym parent.

My daughter was taking a flying trapeze class one summer at the park. During her class, a father approached me with his daughter. He asked about the class for his daughter, who is also a gymnast and had won state championship the last 4 years in a row. Proud dad! My response, "Oh, my daughter's a gymnast too. Your daughter would love the trapeze class". He replied with what could only be described as the inquisition. *How old is she? What level is she now? What level was she last year? What level will she be next year? What gym does she go to? Can she do this or that?* He quickly crossed that line from proud to crazy!

Being Supportive

Student leadership development expert Tim Elmore wrote an article where he discusses his research on what parents can say both before and after the competitions to encourage their kids, without making everything about performance (either positively or negatively). Based on psychological research, the three healthiest statements moms and dads can make are:

Before the Competition:	*After the competition:*
Have fun.	Did you have fun?
Play hard.	I'm proud of you.
I love you.	I love you.

Researchers Bruce Brown and Rob Miller asked college athletes what their parents said that made them feel great and brought them joy when they played sports. Want to know the six words they most want to hear their parents say?

"I love to watch you play."

That says it all and that is all you should say.

Are you a Crazy Gym Parent? Quiz

Everyone should take this quiz from time to time to see how close to the line they are.

Good Luck!

A Parent's Questionnaire
Dr. Alan Goldberg   Competitive Advantage

Take this questionnaire to see if you're doing everything possible to help your child have a successful and healthy sports experience.

Answer each question with a 1, 2, 3 or 4.
1 = never true;
2 = occasionally true;
3 = mostly true;
4 = always true.

_____1) I get really frustrated and upset when my child performs below his/her capabilities.
_____2) I give my child critical feedback on his/her performance after each game.
_____3) If I didn't push my child, he/she wouldn't practice.
_____4) If my child does not excel and win, I see very little point in his participating in the sport.
_____5) I can be very critical when my child makes mistakes or loses.
_____6) I set goals with my child in relation to the sport.
_____7) I think it is my job to motivate my child to get better.
_____8) I feel angry and embarrassed when my child performs poorly.
_____9) The most important thing for my child's sport participation is that he/she have fun.
_____10) I get really upset with bad calls by the officials.
_____11) Most coaches do not know what they are talking about.

_____12) I keep a performance log/journal/statistics on my child's performance so we can monitor his/her progress.

_____13) I feel guilty about some of the things I say to my child after he/she plays.

_____14) I try to watch most practices so that I can correct my child when he makes mistakes.

_____15) When my child fails I can feel his pain and disappointment.

_____16) I think it is important that my child gets used to having coaches yell at him/her to help prepare him/her for life.

_____17) My spouse and I argue about how I treat my son/daughter in relation to his/her sport.

_____18) I try to help my child keep his/her failures and the sport in perspective.

_____19) I'm never very concerned about the outcome of my child's game/match/race.

_____20) I will not allow my child to be put down or yelled at by a coach.

_____21) If my child was not so defensive when it comes to my feedback, he/she could become a better athlete.

_____22) It is not my job to evaluate or criticize my child's performances.

_____23) I feel that my child owes us a certain performance level given all the sacrifices we've made for him/her.

_____24) I believe my child's sport belongs to him/her and not to me.

_____25) I just want my child to feel good about him/herself and be happy when he/she plays.

SCORING

Add scores for questions #1-8, 10-14,16, 17, 21 & 23. (If you answered question #2 with a "mostly true" you add 3 points to the total score.) Subtract scores for questions #9, 15, 18-20, 22, 24, & 25.

INTERPRETATION

The higher the score, the more potential damage that you are doing to your child. High scores indicate that you are playing the wrong role on the team and if you continue, you will increase the chances of your child burning out, struggling with performance problems and dropping out. Low scores mean that you are on track and doing the things necessary to insure that your child has a positive and life-enriching sports experience. If you scored a:

60 – 50: You are doing everything in your power to seriously damage your child's self-esteem, ruin their sports experience and make them a candidate for long term psychotherapy later on in their life. If you continue your ways, your child will most likely drop out of sports. If you force them to continue, chances are good that they will struggle with serious performance problems. On the off chance that they do achieve success, they will not be able to appreciate what they've accomplished. Finally, your long term relationship with them will be seriously jeopardized because of your lack of perspective and behaviors.

49 – 39: You are not being supportive enough and are doing too many things wrong. You are over-involved and putting too much pressure on your child. You need to back down, chill out and let them enjoy their sport. This kind of a parental stance will drive your child out of sports.

38 – 20: You're OK, but you need some help getting unhooked. You need to be more consistently supportive and take less of a pushing/coaching role.

19 – 1: You are pretty much on track as a parent. You are positive and doing most of the right things to insure your child has a positive youth sports experience.

0 - negative 15: BRAVO!!!! You are truly a winning parent. You can give workshops to other parents on how to help your child become successful in their sport.

Now that you've taken Dr. Al Goldberg's test and know how close to the line you are, this is what a group of your peers think. I have surveyed my fellow gym parents and these are TRUE examples of gym parent craziness. Is any single act crazy or is a combination of the below examples crazy? You tell me. Personally, I think if you have done any of these things, you are either a crazy gym parent and you need to dial it back or you are so close to the line you're almost out of bounds.

During Practice

- ⅄ Yelling at your daughter or shouting out technical corrections to your child because "the coach isn't providing enough corrections" disrupting everyone in the gym.

- ⅄ Sitting in the lobby with a stopwatch so you can time the amount of time that each girl is getting on the beam (or bar)....sadly it is a true story.

- ⅄ Giving the coach your expert opinion about where every child on the team should be placed next year.

- ⅄ Getting angry at your child for enjoying her sport and having fun.

- ⅄ Saying anything that resembles "Are you sure you can't push through your back pain to go to practice tonight?" or "Didn't you study enough for your midterm? You have a meet coming up!"

- ⅄ Telling other parents how your daughter is more talented than theirs, and how the coaches love coaching her more than other girls in the gym.

⅄ Asking parents of the top gymnast in your gym what their daughter eats, how many hours of sleep, what music she likes, etc. so you can have your daughter do the same. Or even worse you ask parents of other gyms gymnasts' at meets.

At Home

⅄ Making your child condition or do a dance thru at home, like a chore or as a punishment. This is different from the gymnast that wants to and does not stop.

⅄ Restricting your child's caloric/food intake. Any doctor will tell you that all children should eat a well-balanced diet, restricting what they eat can have serious consequences later on in life. It could lead them down the road of anorexia and/or bulimia. Body image is a very delicate issue at this point in your gymnast's development and constantly monitoring what they put in their mouths may cause unnecessary mental stress. Your child is growing and the work they do in the gym requires an extra caloric intake to maintain healthy muscles, bones, and blood. Lack of food can lead to exhaustion mentally and physically and leave your child open to injuries.

Competitions

⅄ Showing up for a higher level competition with your gymnast all dressed and ready so she can compete because you feel she should be competing a level higher. The answer is going to be no. Putting your coach on the spot will just embarrass you and annoy your coach. We had a parent whose daughter was not old enough to compete yet show up at a meet and attempt to push her into the meet! Needless to say she did not compete and moved onto another gym.

- ⚔ Sitting down with your child pre meet and having a strategy meeting. Reviewing key corrections on each event and then discussing the corrections post meet.

- ⚔ Walking out during a meet, while your daughter is competing, because she is not doing well or storming out of awards because your child did not place.

- ⚔ Getting angry at your gymnast for doing poorly on an event and "ruining" their all around. A 10 year old at level 6 states fell off the beam in the middle of a lovely routine, only to have her mother hiss, "She just RUINED her all-around score!"

- ⚔ Getting angry at a gymnast on your daughters team for not scoring as well as they usually do and "ruining the team's chance at placing". Even worse sharing this feeling / opinion with the parent of that girl.

- ⚔ Do I really need to say it? Stalking is way over the line. Showing up to a meet where your daughter is not competing and videotaping girls who your daughter will eventually face in meets later that season, or worse, telling a parent that you have been tracking their daughter's scores on MyMeetScores.com. As if tracking the gymnast isn't crazy enough!

- ⚔ Yelling at your child on the way home about their performance or punishing your child for a score or bad practice

- Comparing your gymnast's performance to their teammates or any other gymnasts at the meet. Comparing them will probably not inspire them to be better but rather take the enjoyment out of the sport and crush their confidence.

- Analyzing past scores of all kids in your kid's awards group. After each meet you break down placement by whether the kids are repeaters or not. This one stirred up a lot of controversy on whether or not it is crossing the line. It was agreed however sharing that info with your gymnast can mess up their minds and make meets a disaster.

Confession time– At the meet before level 5 states, my daughter did really well and scored very high. Naturally, I was excited for her. I came across MyMeetScores.com and could not resist looking at the potential. According to the website, she was sure to take it all! Thankfully, I did not share this information with her. At states in marched an entire team that looked more like a group of level 7s than 5s! Turns out, they were all in her age division! She did very well and was very proud of herself, and we were proud of her. I never looked at those scores again, and I actually try to pay as little attention as possible to the scores flashed for other gymnasts not on her team.

Non-gym parents

Your daughter is not the only one being judged. It is important to note the definition of a crazy gym parent from the point of view of a non-gym parent is *every single one of us*. You must be a crazy gym parent if: you have a beam in your house, your child goes to the gym more than once a week, your gymnast has her medals on her wall, you have a gymnastics photo on your wall, you post a YouTube video or you even mention gymnastics. I say this for one important reason: no matter what you do, you will have friends and family members tell you that you are crazy. You will learn very quickly who you can and cannot talk to about gymnastics. Sorry, but it is true. You will be judged. Before you get upset, defensive, and angry, stop and ask yourself this question. If you told your gymnast she had to quit gymnastics, what would her reaction be? If your gymnast would move into the gym if allowed, would rather go or do gymnastics than anything else, and you can honestly say your gymnast is doing gymnastics for themselves and not you …you are fine. I often think about my daughter's peers at school. What are they doing? Girl scouts, soccer team, swimming club, karate classes, dance classes, playing video games and sitting on the couch. The difference is my daughter does one activity, which she loves and in which she excels. If she was not at the gym, she would be flipping around the house on the furniture.

Other gym parents

While non-gym parents do not understand, you would think fellow gym parents got your back, right? Not always. Gymnastics is a very different dynamic than other sports because it is both a team and individual sport at the same time. While the girls are competing together as a team simultaneously they could be competing directly against each other. Watch what you say and who you say it to. Seeking support on a community internet board such as ChalkBucket.com without using your name or gym name can be a good anonymous resource. Keep in mind with all internet message boards people tend to speak their minds while hidden behind a keyboard and screen. Try not to take anything personally. I have seen it both on message boards and in person. An innocent conversation unintentionally turns ugly fast. While you may have just been talking about how you feel, another mother may think you are indirectly attacking her. Parents by nature are defensive of their children and their parenting choices. You may indirectly or unknowingly challenge someone making them defensive.

Bribes vs awards

A bribe is an incentive and offered before an event or practice. *If you place at the meet today I will get you a sweatshirt.* An award is offered or gifted afterwards. *Congrats on placing! Let's go buy you a sweatshirt.*

Many parents provide incentives or awards to their gymnast for achieving a skill, overcoming a fear, scoring well or placing. Is it crazy? That depends on if the gymnast's drive is solely based on the award. Your gymnast should be self-motivated and should be pushing and working hard for themselves, because they want it, not because they want the new iPhone. That said, I have both awarded and bribed. When my gymnast was having a mental block, I told her and her coach they would get baked cookies if she did the skill. With the coach's help, she did it. My goal was to take everyone's mind off of the skill and on to the idea of cookies. It worked, for the day. I have purchased the extremely overpriced sweatshirt with all the bells and whistles as an award for coming in first.

While I am at it, let me prepare you for extortion/gambling. I have seen all gymnasts do it or try it. *Hey mom, if I place at States can I have a puppy?* Here is where you need to be careful. I have been suckered into these kinds of agreements. I have actually consulted a coach before practice asking what the chances she's going to do X today. I have had the coach honestly tell me, "not gonna happen" and then the little stinker pulled it off. Thankfully, most of the time our little wagers were ice cream based and don't break the bank. As you find yourself, and you will, in these bribe- award- extortion situations just remember it is all in fun. Don't make it into more.

Gym Parent Stages

This is a somewhat comical classification of gymnastics parents that I have seen on the internet over the years written for different sports and revised by different people. The origin is unknown but here is my version. It is good for a laugh but there is also a lot of truth in it. Stages do not need to be completed in order, parents can experience several stages in one season, and some get stuck for years at a single stage.

Pre Stage: The gymnast is simply happy to be doing gymnastics, but parents are convinced that their child could and should be doing more. Their gymnast is so talented and amazing she must be on team! Parents are so excited with the concept of team that they do not want to miss one second of practice. They watch other groups and are constantly wondering why and how they were broken up and surely their gymnast should be in the most advanced group. If coaches change they are concerned their daughter is in the wrong group. These parents usually only know a handful of skills and are obsessed with "back handsprings" and want to know if they are working on them and when will they do them.

Stage 1: Gymnast and parents are both clueless. It is all fun and games. The novelty comes from wearing a fancy leotard and fancy hair styles with pretty scrunchies. They have no clue about the sport, no concept of how scores are calculated, what skill elements are required, or what routines should look like. Parents are oblivious to other gyms in the area because they chose the one right down the street from the house. The focus is not on winning. Parents are concerned with their own gymnast and whether or not she will make it through the routine without running off the floor crying or having to go to the bathroom.

Stage 2: Gymnast has gained some skills. Parents are starting to learn and understand a little about levels. They are excited and proud that their gymnast has learned some new skills; however, teammates are learning some skills too and the worry sets in about their gymnast keeping up, or falling behind. Parents also start to notice that other gyms in the area have teams that are good and they start to question whether or not their gym is the best gym around. They now know their gymnast will make it through a routine, and they start to crave winning.

Stage 3: Parents are at peak PSYCHO mode. Gymnast has gained more skills, and parents are excited but still nervous because some of gymnast's friends have gained more skills and possibly "tested out of levels" or put into the "fast track" stream. Parents get hard on their gymnast, putting pressure on her to "get better" and work harder in the gym and train even more at home. Parents are starting to understand scoring, know how to look up meet sessions and meet results like a pro, and stalk YouTube videos and message forums to see what her gymnast is up against. They are full-fledged into having their gymnast be a winning gymnast! Parents now knows all the weaknesses of her gymnast's gym, and will take every opportunity to point out those weaknesses! Talk about changing gyms is rampant, unless gymnast's gym has a winning record and their gymnast shines a little brighter than her teammates. Even if it does. there are still issues parents need to complain about and the thoughts about whether the grass is greener at the other gyms sometimes wins out and they move. Complaints about other kids, coaches, methods, parents, etc. is at their peak! These parents are always looking to have a "gymnastics" conversation and when meeting another gym team parent they grill them on what skills they have and their gymnast's level. When two stage 3 or stage 4 parents meet a full-fledged "my gymnast is better than yours" war tends to breaks out.

Stage 4: Parents are still psycho, but gymnast is progressing even more and that is enough to keep parents happy, especially if there was a gym change. Parents are in full-fledged gymnastics mania! They want that win bad! Relationships with other gym parents have developed, even parents from other gyms. They may still be putting tons of pressure on gymnast to fix this and fix that, get this and get that, etc.

Stage 5: Parents still have hidden anxiety, but have stopped telling everyone about it. They have met some stage 3 psycho parents and realize how insanely idiotic they act. They have come to terms with their own gymnast's level and have started taking away the pressures, but still quietly encourage improvement. They enjoy some quiet conversation with other stage 5 & stage 6 gym parents. They fully understand by now what it takes to win, and have accepted that kids develop in different stages. They now also understand that kids have strengths and weaknesses, including their own gymnast, and they all contribute to a team beautifully.

Stage 6: Parents have settled nicely into a happy group of other veteran parents and laugh out loud at the stage 3 parents. They still want to win, but they now realize that winning is not everything. They have found peace with their gymnast, and they give her the tools she needs to succeed, but they no longer push so hard. This peace continues through the rest of gymnast's gym career.

The "can't look" stage can be combined with any of the other stages. At this stage, the gymnast is starting to work on skills that scare the parents. These parents are afraid of phone calls from the gym during practice and have a lot of anxiety watching not only their daughter, but all the gymnasts at the meet. These parents need to be very careful not to influence their gymnast or they can make her insecure.

The "whatever" stage is when the parents drop off, pick up and pay. They have no interest in anything that goes on in the gym and seldom attend competitions. These gymnasts rely on coaches and other parents for help and support. There is no question that these gymnasts are dedicated and doing it for themselves. Before you judge these parents, sometimes there are other siblings, work obligations, health issues, etc. These may also be burned out stage 3 parents.

CHAPTER 8
PROBLEMS

Conflicts

It is not all rainbows and unicorns. Gymnastics can be stressful and frustrating for everyone involved. Over time, you are bound to have disagreements or difficulty with coaches, other parents, or between teammates. Here are a few guidelines on how to handle these circumstances.

It sounds cliché, but no matter who the difficulty is with you should take a minute and think before you say or do something you will regret. Try to take 24 hours. In 24 hours hopefully, everyone is able to step back and reflect on the situation before anyone over reacts.

Coaches

Remember coaches are human and doing their best to do a job. If, after 24 hours you are still unhappy with a situation with a coach, your first step is to try to talk to him / her directly. Depending on the situation you may or may not want your gymnast present for the discussion. I recommend the first discussion to happen without the gymnast regardless of the situation. If you are still not satisfied with the situation, speak to the head coach. There are exceptions to this, see later in this chapter abuse vs motivation.

Parents

Problems with other parents are a little more delicate. Again, take those 24 hours and think. Parents are looking out for their child, just like you are looking out for yours. I have often compared dealing with other mothers to Junior High School.

Do not take it personally and try your best to walk away and separate yourself. A coach's job is to coach your child not to referee parents. Do not drag your coaches or the kids into these problems. Remember, we are all adults and this is not Junior High.

Teammates

Girls will be girls. Be careful when dealing with problems between gymnasts. Best friends one day, sworn enemies the next and back to best buds again. Do not get me wrong there can be real problems. Talk to your gymnast and do not jump to conclusions. If, after counseling your gymnast, things are not getting better or you feel it is interfering with practice or meets, try talking to the coach. The coaches spend a lot of time with the group and may be able to shed light on problems and resolve them. As a last resort you can talk to the other parent. Again remember any parent will defend their own child. You may find out they think your child is the problem not theirs and now there is a problem between gymnasts and parents! Let cooler heads prevail.

Abuse vs. Motivation

"The wise coach develops not only the fullest physical potential in his charges, but also those capacities and habits of mind and body which will enrich and ennoble their later years."
(Geoffrey Dyson speaking to the 19th session of the International Olympic Academy, Greece 1979)

There is a line between abusive and motivational in the athlete / coach relationship. There are parents that feel as long as the gymnast is winning anything the coach says or does is fine with them. On the flip side if a gymnast is not winning I have heard parents demand their child be yelled at or disciplined by the coach. So where is that line? Is it in the language used? Is it in the intent? Is it in the effect it has on the gymnast?

This is probably one of the hardest topics in gymnastics, or any sport. First we need to remember that coaches are human. They lose their patience and may say things they do not mean or regret, just like we do as parents. They are not perfect. We need to learn the difference between a bad day and a bad coach.

I have seen coaches at meets in a public arena, a place I would think they are on their "best behavior" and can only wonder, how do they behave in private at practice? or   when no one is looking or listening? If they are *this* mean with ears and eyes on them…I cringe at the thought. Winning is never worth the damage a mean and abusive coach can do to a child's spirit.

An abusive coach is a bully, plain and simple. They use threats and fear to scare athletes into submission. They destroy a child's self-esteem and undermine their confidence.

Demeaning kids is not coaching. Ask yourself honestly, if another child was speaking to your child or treating your child that way, would you think it was ok? What coaches say and how they say it should be constructive and age-appropriate. Do not hesitate to talk to the coach if you observe behavior that appears hurtful, demeaning or abusive.

Dr. Goldberg, a known expert in sports psychology wrote: *"When a coach is emotionally abusive you are faced with a very difficult situation. You're walking a political and emotional tightrope. If you do nothing, your child is at risk of having his self-esteem further traumatized and his joy of the sport killed. However, if you say or do something, you risk the coach retaliating and punishing your daughter even more. You also might get labeled as a pushy, over-involved parent. My feeling: Trying to keep the peace and not rocking the boat is not worth the emotional damage that your child will sustain remaining in this kind of abusive situation. I urge all parents to blow the whistle on abusive coaches. There is NEVER an excuse for adults in a position of power to demean, embarrass and humiliate our children. NEVER!!! This is NOT education! This is NOT coaching. It is, instead, inexcusable behavior.*

"That is just the way it is", "why even try?" BECAUSE all kids deserve to be in a safe and positive environment. These are lifetime injuries and they change kids forever. Our athletic careers are just a drop of water, in the bucket of life. Hopefully, we have a great coach who has helped form us into a well-rounded, hardworking, team player who has the self-confidence to change the athletic world for the better. Be your child's advocate. Say, "NO" to abuse."

CHAPTER 9
TAKING CARE OF YOUR GYMNAST

Stretching and conditioning at home on days off is not always a great idea. The body needs to rest. Most gyms have a conditioning schedule that alternates body parts giving muscles time to recuperate and heal. If your gymnast wants to add an at home exercise regimen ask the coach. There may be a safe drill they can do at home or they can tell you which exercises to avoid. You want to avoid overuse injuries and burn out.

Nutrition & Overall Health

Years ago coaches used to track a gymnast's weight by having weigh-ins at the gym. This practice created insecure, self-conscience, unhealthy girls that struggle their entire lives with eating disorders. There are many books written about and by Elite gymnasts detailing this horrible practice and abuse. The sport has changed. If your gym weighs gymnasts, you need to stand up for the sake of your child. Do not allow anyone to make your child feel insecure. This is not an acceptable or appropriate practice.

It is best to think of a gymnast's body as a machine and food is fuel. Thin and light is NOT ideal for a gymnast, and a gymnast should not watch the scale. Gymnasts need muscle mass – muscle weighs more than fat. My pediatrician always looks twice at my daughter's weight at checkups and I constantly have to remind them when prescribing medication. She is solid muscle.

Gymnastics is physically demanding relying on physical and mental well-being. A balanced, healthy diet is needed to help develop and maintain lean muscles. Carbohydrates for energy, protein for muscles and healthy fats are essential, as well as calcium for bone health. Make sure your gymnast understands the importance of nutrition and eating. Thin and light is not better, strength and endurance are key. The most powerful tumblers I have seen are broad and muscular, not sticks. They work their bodies hard and as such need, more calories/fuel than a child that plays video games. My daughter's team has been at my house many times over the years, and I am always shocked by how much those little bodies eat!

A coach once said to me that he can always tell when a gymnast is about to have a growth spurt they suddenly look a little wide, then shoot up a few inches and thin back out. Puberty brings body changes and each growth spurt presents challenges to the gymnast. Their reach and length change may require them to re-learn the feel of a skill. Be patient. It will all fall back into place...until the next spurt!

Snacks at meets and in the gym. You should try to avoid nuts at meets and in the gym. Nut allergies are becoming more common and are very dangerous. A gymnast can unintentionally and very easily contaminate the beam or other equipment. It is a misconception that a food has to be digested for someone to have a reaction. Especially with nuts just coming in contact with a trace can send someone to the hospital. Instead focus on quick, easy, and healthy. Snack options are zip lock bags with dry cereal or granola, yogurt, fruits, crackers, and veggie sticks.

Staying hydrated is very important for athletes. Avoid coffee, tea, sugary fruit punches, caffeine and carbonated drinks. Pure water, pure fruit juices and sports drinks are the best way to stay hydrated.   To remain hydrated, gymnasts should drink before, during, and after gymnastics practice.

Dan Benardot, PhD, DHC, RD, LD, FACSM is Full Professor of Nutrition and Director of the Laboratory for Elite Athlete Performance at Georgia State University. He was one of the founding members of the Athlete Wellness Committee for USA Gymnastics and was the first American appointed to the Medical Commission of the international governing body for gymnastics (FIG). Dr Dan Benardot wrote: *"Gymnastics activity involves short bursts of high-intensity activity so gymnasts have a high requirement for carbohydrate, the primary muscle fuel for this type of work. Because our bodies do not store much. Gymnasts should take every opportunity to consume carbohydrates during meals and snacks. Recent studies have demonstrated that athletes performing high-intensity activities similar to gymnastics gain a performance benefit if sports drinks, such as Gatorade. Are used during breaks in the activity. In addition. Gymnasts should eat a wide variety of foods that provide a balance of nutrients. While the focus of the foods consumed should be high in carbohydrates (breads. cereals, fruits, vegetables and legumes), be sure to include foods that are good sources of protein and also some fats, which carry the fat-soluble vitamins A, D. E and K. Meat (beef, chicken, fish. pork) is an excellent source of protein. Iron and zinc, all of which are important nutrients for staying healthy and maintaining a high level of athletic performance. Limit the intake of fried foods, high-fat dairy products, prepared meats (hot dogs, salami, bologna. etc.) and visible fats (butter, margarine, fatty meats. etc.).*

Gymnasts should eat and enjoy everything else and remember that eating a wide variety of foods is key to maintaining good health and peak performance. "

Dr Dan Benardot recommends: What to Eat for the…

Big Competition / Pre-Practice/Competition:

Gymnasts should have a small high-carbohydrate snack about one hour prior to practice or competition, and should drink water or a sports drink prior to training. Frequent drinking is a good strategy for maintaining gymnastics performance.

During Practice/Competition:

Gymnasts should develop the habit of consuming 4-6 ounces of a sports drink every 10 to 15 minutes during practice and competition. This helps to meet the needs of both carbohydrate, which muscles use up quickly during gymnastics performance, and fluids, which are key to maintaining muscle function.

Post-Practice/Competition:

Having a high-carbohydrate snack (crackers, bread, banana. energy bar, etc.) immediately following practice or competition helps the body restore the carbohydrate in the muscles so the muscles are ready to do more activity on the following day This is also a good time to encourage gymnasts to drink plenty of fluids

Rips

Coaches and gymnasts joke that you are not a real gymnast until you rip. A rip is caused by the friction of the bars against the palm of the hand or fingers. The skin blisters and then rips. It is painful but normally does not require a visit to the doctor's office. There are many different thoughts on the care of rips. Some recommend using Preparation H cream or black tea bags on the rips. I have even heard of soaking a rip in pickle juice to help speed up the healing process. Fragrance-free lotion or vitamin E oil will stop the fresh skin underneath from cracking or in a pinch, black classic chap-stick or Vaseline work as well.

No matter how you plan to treat the rip the first few steps are always the same. Cut off excessive skin, wash, and treat with anti-bacterial cream. Rips are a fact of life for a gymnast and usually heal without any problem; however, if the rip appears to get worse a visit to the doctor may be warranted.

When my daughter rips or is getting a rip, we use the oil from a Vitamin E capsule on the rip and place a sock or cotton glove over it every night until it is healed. This also works great on peeling feet along with a vitamin enriched cream. Gross, but no one said gymnastics was glamorous!

After a gymnast has their first rip, it is common for the gymnast and/or parent to request grips. Grips are strips of leather made to cover the palm of the gymnast's hand. Never go out and purchase grips on your own and trust your coach to know when the gymnast will need them. Every gym has different philosophy on the usage of grips and there are several types.

While you are waiting for the green light for grips you can purchase athletic tape and someone at your gym should be able to make what they call "tape grips" to provide a little relief. You can also google "tape grips" for instructional videos and instructions to make them yourself.

Injuries

Gymnastics is a dangerous sport. I will not address the endless number of injuries and problems but rather a few very common overuse injuries. Overuse injuries are from long hours of practice and the wear and tear on the joints. If your gymnast is having an ongoing issue or severe pain the best bet is to see a pediatric orthopedist as soon as possible. A sports pediatric orthopedist is the best bet as they will understand both common growth plate issues and common sports overuse issues. They also tend to be more sensitive to the gymnasts desire to be in the gym.

I know a gymnast that was experiencing discomfort and went to an orthopedist who told her and her mother that she just did not have the body for gymnastics and as skills got harder she would have more pain. You can imagine this statement was devastating to a child who was just told that any hope she had of advancing in gymnastics is gone and that she was not going to be able to return to the gym. Thankfully they got a second opinion. The pediatric sports orthopedist explained that yes, her condition was not ideal for gymnastics but with physically therapy there was no reason why she could not continue and have a successful gymnastics career.

Ankles / Wrists
A gymnast's ankles and wrists take a beating. Many gymnasts, as they get older, need ankle braces or tiger paws for their wrists. This is especially true of gymnasts that tumble off the spring floor on hard surfaces, such as grass.

Knees / Feet

Osgood-Schlatter Disease (OSD) is an overuse injury and one of the most common causes of knee pain. Growth spurts make kids vulnerable because their bones, muscles, and tendons are growing quickly and not always at the same time. With exercise, differences in size and strength between the muscle groups place unusual stress on the growth plate at the top of the shinbone. They make several braces and straps to help ease the pressure and inflammation.

Sever's disease, a common heel injury in kids, is due to inflammation (swelling) of the growth plate in the heel. There are several heel cups and straps on the market to help with severs and I think my daughter has tried them all. There are also stretches for the arch of the foot that eases up the strain on the growth plate.

Do NOT play doctor. It is always a good idea to get an orthopedist's opinion. X-rays and MRIs will confirm diagnosis. While OSD & Severs are painful they are not damaging in the long run and resolve themselves with ice, stretching and braces. You never know if there is something more serious going on and catching a hairline fracture before it becomes a break is a good thing.

Neck and Back issues

Neck and low-back pain in gymnasts related to muscular strain or ligament sprain usually responds to rest and physical therapy exercises. Any ongoing neck / back issues or severe pain is not common and should be checked out as soon as possible.

RICE - Rest / Ice / Compress / Elevate

The rule of thumb after an athletic injury is R.I.C.E.

Rest: Activity should be reduced.

Ice: Ice will reduce pain and swelling and should be applied for 15-20 minutes and removed for 45-60 minutes before being applied again.

Compression: Compression should be applied lightly in the form of an elastic wrap so that it accommodates swelling. Anytime the wrap seems too tight or causes swelling below the wrap it should be loosened.

Elevation: Holding the injured part above the level of the heart is standard treatment to reduce swelling.

CHAPTER 10
MENTAL HEALTH

The dreaded mental block!

A mental block occurs when a gymnast suddenly and inexplicably stops doing a skill they previously had no difficulty performing. The gymnast usually has no idea why their body will not move. It is a subconscious, involuntary response. I have seen many gymnasts stand on the beam prepared to do a backhand spring and not move. Beam height, full spot, additional mats, nothing seems to help. They just cannot go, they cannot move. It is not the gymnast's choice and no one is more frustrated than they are in that moment. This is not uncommon. Once your child experiences one, mental blocks are easy to spot at every meet by the look of frustration on the child's and coach's faces.

My daughter started doing a flyaway dismount from bars when she was a 7 year old bronze level gymnast. As an 11 year old level 7, she just stopped. One day, with no warning she just stopped letting go of the bar. No amount of coaxing could get her to let go. The coach would grab her by the waist and hold her, all she had to do was let go and she could not let go.

Dr Goldberg explains," The most important thing to mammals, and above all else, we are still animals, is survival. And our nervous systems are programmed so that when they detect danger, they will reflexively click into self-protective response. Now most of us know this as fight or flight. However, when a gymnast is on the beam getting ready to go backwards or on the floor ready to begin a back tumbling pass, she can't fight and she can't really flee. And when any mammal is in danger and can't protect themselves by fighting or fleeing, there's a third, default survival option that clicks in: the freeze or immobility response. Suddenly the gymnast can't get herself to go."

" What they need from you in both your words and behaviors is to know that your love is unconditional, that you are not overly invested in their performance and frustrated by it. They need to know from you that their happiness and emotional wellbeing is more important to you than how well they do in the gym!

When you can communicate this unconditional love and acceptance to them, you will help them feel safer inside and this will help lower their nervous system's danger response that is feeding the balking. "

"Remember, your child is not afraid on purpose. They really want to get through this block. Your job is to help them feel safer in the process. To help them understand that you wholeheartedly support and love them. To help them feel your patience. And to give them the message that they will eventually get through this and that they need to be patient and kind to themselves in the process."

Helping your gymnast with nerves

A gymnast can become overwhelmed with "what if's". It is common for a gymnasts to be so focused and anxious about an event or skill that every event/skill they compete leading up to it is affected. For example a gymnast worried about her backhand spring on beam may be unable to focus on bars or fall off the beam on a simple skill just before the backhand in the routine.

Dr. Goldberg advises athletes to get a constructive handle on the "what if's". He wrote: You have to develop an awareness of when you mentally leave the NOW and jump ahead into the future. When that happens, you want to immediately return your concentration to the task at hand in the moment. By staying mentally in the NOW, you will calm yourself down and keep your muscles loose enough so that they will work as trained whenever the pressure of competition is turned up high.

You may not be able to completely stop the "what if's" from beginning to play in your head. That is okay! Your job is to quickly notice those first few familiar stanzas of the "what if'" song and then, just as quickly, bring yourself back to what you're doing in the NOW.

Remember, a future focus of concentration always feeds fear and nervousness. Discipline yourself to stay in the NOW before and during your competitions. This is the key to staying calm and composed when it counts the most.

Concentrating on your opponent and obsessing about winning will do a lot of things for you. It will get you overly nervous. It will erode your self-confidence. It will psych you out. It will guarantee that you play poorly. It will contribute to your losing to this particular opponent. It will always leave you frustrated and disappointed after the game. However, what it will never do for you is increase your chances of performing to your potential.

If you're hung up on winning and losing, and too worried about your opponent beating you, then listen up! You have this competition thing all wrong! If your goals are to win or to beat someone else you're setting yourself up to fail. It is not about the competition. It is about you! Let me explain:

The father of legendary UCLA basketball coach, John Wooden used to tell his Hall of Fame son, "never try to be better than someone else, but never cease trying to be the best that YOU can be." The true purpose of sport and competition is to put yourself in a situation where you try to push your own envelope, where you try to excel based on your own abilities and potential. Real winning, in other words, is NOT about the outcome of the match or game. It is about whether you played to the very best of your abilities.

Being a champion means that you go out every day and compete against yourself. It requires that you stop getting hung up on the uncontrollable and misplaced goal of winning, and instead focus on playing like a winner. It requires that you focus on playing your own game instead of allowing your opponent or the game importance to dictate how you play. It means striving to be the best that YOU can be.

Check out Dr Goldberg's blog and at resources www.competitivedge.com

Spectator Nerves

It is natural to be nervous or anxious for your child. Not only do you want her to do well but watching your child flip on a 2 inch beam two feet in the air can be stressful. Unintentionally, I find myself holding my breath while my daughter competes beam or does a move that she is struggling with. I have fellow gym parents that have to leave the room. While It Is natural, I think you need to be careful not to let your gymnast see or feel your anxiety. They know what they are doing.

Nastia Lukin's mom, an Olympic athlete herself, was said not to be able to watch her daughter compete and at the Olympics was shown covering her face while her daughter competed.

My favorite example is a video that can be found on YouTube. It is video of Aly Raisman competing on bars at the 2012 London Olympics. During the routine, her parents are shown sitting in the stands moving along with her, leaning right and leaning left. The video says it all.

Personally, I like to record all of my daughter's competitions, not just to have them to show off to family or reminisce. The act of videotaping or photography can calm the nerves.

CHAPTER 11
EXPECTATIONS AND GOALS

Expectations vs Goals

According to Dr. Jim Taylor, psychologist and author of *Positive Pushing: How to Raise a Successful and Happy Child*, goals are possible accomplishments that may or may not be achieved, yet can provide satisfaction to children just by going through the process of setting them and trying to attain them. Expectations, on the other hand, are all or nothing; they are assumptions of achievement.

As previously discussed, a gymnast should always strive to do their best but should never expect to win. I have seen the expectation to win crush a gymnast at a bad meet. Everyone eventually has a bad meet. You cannot win every time, and no one should expect to win every time. You hope, you work hard, you do your best, but you never know what will happen and you do not always know your competition. Gymnasts are very competitive by nature and very hard on themselves. If parents are not careful, they can easily feed into these expectations. When a parent expects a gymnast to place, score well, and win, it only sets the gymnast up to feel like a failure and damages their self-esteem.

Over-confidence

Hard work beats talent when talent does not work hard. I have seen it time and time again: A very talented gymnast wins at every meet, skills come easy and they become lazy and arrogant. They do not need to practice; they are the best no matter what they do. Eventually, other gymnasts catch up and that talented gymnast stops placing. Without the win gymnastics isn't fun anymore and she quits.

I knew a gymnast that was extremely talented. She seemed to fly through the levels placing each step of the way. She got accustomed to everything coming easy. She would goof off, miss practices and hang out in the office. When she hit level 9, it required more effort and more work, and it was no longer fun. Other girls working hard caught up, she walked away from the sport.

What can you do? Success in gymnastics should not be measured by meet placement. Help your gymnast set realistic goals outside of competition scores and award placement and support and celebrate improvement and achievements outside of competition.

Goals

Time to set some goals. A goal is something trying to be achieved. First goal for parents is to "let go". Give your gymnast her sport. Let her set her own goals with the help of her coach. Encourage without pressure. Support without expectation.

Setting goals gives the gymnast long-term vision and short-term motivation. The gymnast can measure progress and take pride in each step.

S.M.A.R.T. is a widely-used acronym that stands for

Specific – goal should be as specific as possible

Measurable – goal should be measurable for an indicator of progress

Achievable / Action Orientated – goal should be attainable not far fetched

Realistic –can the goal realistically be achieved?

Time-related – Assign a timeframe to the goal. Time frames should be flexible!

Be S.M.A.R.T. about setting goals.

Set performance goals, not outcome goals. Personal performance goals are in the gymnast's control. No one can control score or placement but a gymnast can control their attitude, work ethic, and focus.

Set realistic goals – It is important for a gymnast to set goals they can achieve. Large and difficult goals should be broken down into smaller, more attainable goals. For example, a common goal for a gymnast is to move up to the next level. That can be a huge undertaking. A level placement goal can be dissected by event, skill and then even conditioning required for the skill. Perhaps she needs a skill on bars to move up and that skill requires the gymnast to increase shoulder strength. With the help of the coach the gymnast can set a conditioning goal such as a specific number of push-ups. Goals should be not just attainable but measurable. Who does not like to cross things off the to-do list? It is a great feeling of accomplishment and increases self-esteem.

Olympic Bound!?

Every gymnast dreams of going to the Olympics and what parent or coach does not want that for their gymnast?

Let's talk numbers. There are approximately 90,000 gymnasts registered in the USAG Junior Olympic program. According to the USAG there are around 28 Junior & Senior Elite members. Now take into consideration who will be the correct age (16 or turning 16 in a summer Olympic year). For example, the 2012 Olympic Trials had 14 girls competing for 5 spots on the Olympic team & 3 alternate spots. My intention is to not discourage anyone's dreams and goals but to help parents maintain reasonable expectations.

Other goals and dreams can include Junior High School, High School and College Gymnastics. Let's not forget about the possibility of scholarships! Again these are hopes and goals, not expectations.

CHAPTER 12
GYMNASICS ORGANIZATIONS

Pre team / Prep team, Mini team

Most gyms have some kind of pre-team, prep-team, mini-team, or advanced class designed to help a gymnast transition from classes to team. These groups usually consist of gymnasts who are missing key elements needed to compete or who are too young to compete at the lowest level offered by that gym. The name of the group varies by gym and works differently everywhere, but in almost all cases, a gymnast has to be invited or has to try-out for these groups.

Levels

There are compulsory and optional levels which refers to the type of routines the level competes.

"Compulsory" level routines are created by USA Gymnastics (USAG). Every gymnast in the country competes the exact same routines.   USAG does give several floor music choices per compulsory level, but the moves are identical. USAG feels this helps gymnasts develop a strong foundation. Note the gym decides on the version of music.

"Optional" levels the gym chooses the music and create their own routines. All optional gymnastics levels require the gymnasts to perform a certain number of skills. These skills are assigned an element value of A through E, with A being basic beginner skills and E being the most advanced skills. These are defined in the organization's code of points. Every level has guidelines as to what skills are permitted, and there are penalties for performing skill designated as too difficult for the level.

It is common for gymnasts from a gym to have the same routines for the first optional level. Some gyms do this to help reduce costs and ease the group into individual routines. If your gym does this do not be mad. Take a minute and consider the money your gym is hopefully saving you. Optional gymnasts must purchase their music, usually from a company that specifically creates floor music; then the gymnast must pay for choreography and gym private time to learn the routine. When a group has the same routine the music is usually provided and the group can learn the routine together during regular gym time or during a clinic.

Gymnastics Organizations

USA Gymnastics (USAG) is the sole national governing body for the sport of gymnastics in the United States. This designation comes from the U.S. Olympic Committee, and the International Gymnastics Federation (FIG). USAG sets the rules and policies that govern gymnastics in the United States including but not limited to selecting and training the U.S. Gymnastics Teams. USAG levels are 1-10 & Elite. Currently, all USAG levels 5 and under are compulsory. Levels 1-3 are designed as non-competitive and achievement-oriented, or used as an introductory to competition. Levels 4 & 5 are progressive in nature, building upon the skills required at the previous level.   Level 6 and over are "optionals". Levels 6, 7, 8, and 9 have difficulty restrictions, while Level 10 has no restrictions in the skill choice.

United States Association of Independent Gymnastics Clubs (USAIGC) and Xcel Gymnastics are both flexible programs designed for gymnasts that have other interests or cannot be in the gym as much for monetary or scheduling reasons. They have all optional levels allowing more flexibility in routines and skills, and have less practice hours than USAG. There are many reasons to choose USAIGC / Xcel over USAG. Some participants want more non-gym time for social reasons or other sport involvement. Others are unable to keep up with the USAG practice time requirements to compete at higher levels or they are unable to meet rigid level skill requirements. Some gyms will use these programs for USAG gymnasts who are between levels.

Xcel vs USAIGC

"The Xcel Program is designed to offer a broad-based, affordable competitive experience outside the traditional Jr. Olympic Program to attract and retain a diverse group of athletes." -USAG

"Competitively, the USAIGC went in a different direction and decided to take a long and more difficult road. A major change was needed. The USAIGC created an OPTIONAL ONLY College Bound Competitive Program using the NCAA Rules for our highest competitive levels and building the foundation to our overall competitive program from these rules creating an Independent Program that stands on its own." - USAIGC

The main difference between Xcel and USAIGC is event competition. In Xcel, a gymnast must compete all events in the same division (Bronze, Silver, Gold, Platinum, or Diamond). In USAIGC, the gymnast that has one or two stronger events can "specialize" and compete those events one level higher than which she competes the weaker events. For instance, when my daughter competed USAIGC Bronze she was able to compete her more advanced skills on floor and beam as Silver. USAIGC feels this prevents frustration for a gymnast. Take for example a gymnast that is weak on beam, balance is just not there but she can rock floor and bars... she just can't stay on the beam. Rather than have that gymnast get frustrated or feel "stuck" in a level, they get to compete up where they excel while they continue to compete all around in the lower level.

Ages

Every level has a minimum age to compete. A gymnast must be at least this age at the time of competition. There is no maximum age listed in any organization for any level.

USAG (USAG 2013-2014 rules & policies)	Level 1	4 years old
	Level 2	5 years old
	Level 3	6 years old
	Levels 4-7	7 years old
	Levels 8-9	8 years old
	Level 10	9 years old
Xcel (USAG Xcel 2013-2014 rules)	Bronze	5 years old
	Silver	6 years old
	Gold	7 years old
	Platinum	8 years old
	Diamond	9 years old
USAIGC (USAIGC 2013-2015 rules & policies)	Copper	5 years old
	Bronze	6 years old
	Silver	7 years old
	Gold	8 years old
	Platinum	9 years old
	Premier	9 years old

Mobility Rules

There are rules governing the move from level to level in all organizations. A gymnast can score out of a level or petition into a level. Note: petitions can *only* be filed by gyms! You cannot petition for your child. Remember there are rules by organization AND each gym has their own standards. Even if your gymnast is permitted to move to the next level according to the organization's rules, your gym may have additional requirements. Teams do not usually advance as a group. Each gymnast progresses at their own rate.

Levels are not like grades at school. A level a year should not be expected. Not only is it common to repeat a level but it can be beneficial. A second year, especially at a lower level, allows the gymnast time to clean up skills and develop nice lines on basic skills that will benefit them later on. Rushing thru levels focusing only on obtaining skills makes for a sloppy higher level gymnast. When repeating a level 2 or 3 times it is important for the gymnast to up-train to avoid getting bored. This is where the gymnast spend some time working on skills for the next level.

In optional levels a gymnast can add and switch out skills without having to move up a level. USAIGC allows a gymnast to move up in 1 or 2 stronger events while staying in the lower level for all around.

If you are concerned about your gymnast's progression arrange a meeting with the coach to discuss their plan.

Moving Up	
USAG *(USAG 2013-2014 rules & policies)*	There are no mobility scores and pre-requisites for levels 1-4 Levels 5-10 have minimum mobility score at the previous level. Only exception is level 6, which can be skipped with level 5 mobility score requirement. A gymnast can compete in a maximum of 2 levels per season.
Xcel *(USAG Xcel 2013-2014 rules)*	Bronze thru Gold mobility is at coach's discretion. There are mobility score requirements for moves from Platinum to Diamond.
USAIGC *(USAIGC 2013-2015 rules)*	Mobility is at the coach's discretion

Dropping Back	
USAG *(USAG 2013-2014 rules & policies)*	Once a gymnast competes at a sanctioned meet, they cannot drop back same season. If the gymnast does not qualify for states, they can petition to drop back next season. Once a gymnast competes at states no drop back is permitted.
Xcel *(USAG Xcel 2013-2014 rules)*	Same as USAG.
USAIGC *(USAIGC 2013-2015 Rules)*	A coach can petition a gymnast to drop back a level prior to the gymnast's second competition. Once a gymnast competes a level at the world championship they cannot drop back.

TOPS

TOPs (Talent Opportunity Program), is an USAG talent search and educational program for female gymnasts ages 7-10 and their coaches. During the months of June and July gymnasts ages 7-10 are evaluated on physical abilities at the state or regional level. These dates are set by the state TOP manager in conjunction with the National TOP Manager. From there, athletes are invited to participate in the National TOP test that is conducted in the month of October where they are evaluated on the same physical abilities tests along with some basic gymnastics skills. Athletes are then invited to participate in the National TOP Training camp which takes place in December of each year. TOPs is not required to progress in gymnastics and is an optional training program done in conjunction with team / level training. TOPs testing involves timed runs, rope climbs, leg lifts, handstands, casts and flexibility to name a few.

Junior Varsity, Varsity, College

While club gymnastics (USAG, USAIGC & Xcel) have levels and age divisions. School gymnastics have Divisions I, II, III and "club".

The National Federation of State High School Associations uses the USAG JO Code of Points and level 9 rules.

The National Collegiate Athletic Association (NCAA) uses the Junior Olympic (JO) Women's Code of Points Requirements (Level 10) modified. NCAA colleges are rated Division 1, 2 and 3 per the NCAA. Division 1 schools have full gym scholarships, Division 2 schools have a few scholarships, and Division 3 schools have teams, but no scholarships for gymnastics.

National Association of Intercollegiate Gymnastics Clubs (NAIGC) uses the USAG JO Code of Points and level 9 rules. No scholarships.

CHAPTER 13

IN THE KNOW

What your coach wants you to know

- ➢ Get your gymnast to the meet on time and prepared.

- ➢ Take responsibility for promoting your gym's reputation. Never make negative comments about other gyms, coaches, gymnasts, or judges. As a Team parent you also represent your gym.

- ➢ Be positive at all times! Set a good example for your gymnast! It may require extra work sometimes, but your attitude will determine your child's attitude.

- ➢ If you have concerns or comments about the meet, see your gymnast's coach at their next practice or email the gym.

- ➢ Once you say goodbye to your gymnast before warm-ups she is the coach's responsibility. Please do not plan to meet or talk to you gymnast during the competition.

What the judges want you to know

- ➤ *Judges do not have it in for certain gymnasts or gyms.*

- ➤ *It may feel "personal" but it really isn't.*

- ➤ *If there is seating near the judges; remember they are concentrating – please be quiet and NEVER try to get their attention for ANY reason*

- ➤ *If you happen to see a judge on the way out after a meet making small talk is ok but never try to discuss scores and deductions.*

There are great resources available on the great World Wide Web! Here are just a few of my personal favorites. Word of advice when joining a message board it is always best to choose a user name that cannot be traced back to you or your gym. This way you can anonymously post questions and concerns without it getting back to the wrong person or group.

www.chalkbucket.com

www.competitivedge.com

www.dbaathletics.com

www.foodandsport.com

www.gymsupply.com

www.headgames.ws

www.ten-o.com

www.usagym.org

www.usaigc.com

Glossary of Terms

Reading this won't make you an expert but may help you understand what your gymnasts is talking about. The USAG website is an amazing resource for all things gymnastics.

A

Aerial: A skill performed without hands. For example; Side Aerial is a cartwheel with no hands, Front Aerial is a front walkover with no hands

Age Requirements: There are minimum age requirements to compete in gymnasts for each level.

All-Around: All Around = All 4 events. An "all around" gymnast competes on all events. "All around" score is the sum of the scores on all events.

Apparatus: Equipment used in gymnastics. For example Beam, Bars

Arabian: A move where the gymnast starts backwards does a half turn in the air and then completes a front flip

Arch: Body position where the hips are pushed forward & the back muscles are contracted.

B

Back Bend: Starting standing upright with arms straight up by the head the gymnasts look at their hands and bend backward until their hands touch the ground and they are in a bridge position.

Back Bend Kick Over: Starting standing upright with arms straight up by the head the gymnasts look at their hands and bend backward until their hands touch the ground and they are in a bridge position. From the Bridge position the gymnast kicks their legs over their head one at a time and land on their on their feet in the lunge position.

Back Extension Roll: From a standing position, gymnast squats down to backwards roll, arms extended as they hit the floor and legs shoot up through a candlestick into a handstand.

Back Handspring Step-out: Jump backwards onto hands through side split and land one foot at a time.

Back Handspring: Jump backwards onto hands and land on two feet. Also referred to as a Flip-Flop or Flic-Flac.

Back Layout Step-out: Jump backwards hands free through side split and land one foot at a time.

Back Straddle: On uneven bars, a gymnast swings backwards straddling their legs, releasing the high bar with flight over the low bar. Finishing by catching the low bar and a kip

Back Tuck: Take off two feet rotates backwards, with knees into chest, then lands again on the feet. Also called Back Salto, Back Somersault.

Back Walkover: Starting on one leg, the gymnast arches back onto hands and passing through a handstand position in a side split by bringing one foot, then the other over the top and stepping down from the handstand into a lunge.

Backward Roll: Starting upright in a standing position the gymnasts squats down onto their heels then rolls backwards pushing off the ground with their hands landing back onto their feet

Block: "Block" is a rapid rebounding off of a flat surface from the shoulders exploding towards extension.

Bounders: Any tumbling skill where two flight moves are executed consecutively.

Bridge: The bridge starting position is on the back, hands next to the head with fingertips pointing toward the toes. Gymnasts bend their legs and place their feet on the floor and push with their arms and legs to end with arms straight and head off the ground.

C

Candlestick: Gymnast is inverted with toes pointing towards the ceiling. On the floor the gymnast's shoulders on the floor while their butt and legs are straight overhead.

Cartwheel: The gymnast moves sideways (like the wheel of a cart) in a straight line alternately placing the hands and then feet on the ground and finishing with the body coming up to a lunge landing position.

Cast: From a front support gymnast swings legs backward while leaning over the bar so that their hips are no longer touching

Cast to Handstand: The gymnast starts in a front support with hips touching the bar - and the gymnast then casts her legs up until reaching a handstand position. Preferable done with straight arms and legs

Chalk: Magnesium carbonate. A tub of powdered chalk or a block is available for gymnasts to place on their hands and/or feet to absorb sweat and improve their grip strength during events especially bars & beams

Clear Hip Circle: A back hip circle in which the gymnast's hips do not touch the bar. Also called a FREE HIP

Closed Position: Whenever a joint is bent, such as in a tuck, when the knees and hips are bent.

Code of Points: An official rulebook for judging gymnastics skills with the rules in which the scoring system and the composition of a program are based. The code of points specifies the difficulty value of all skills, as well as outlines requirements that must be fulfilled for each event. It is a necessary and valuable tool for coaches and judges.

Compulsory: Lower levels where each gymnast across the country compete identical routines created by the USAG

Conditioning: Includes flexibility, strength and endurance training and should be part of every practice session

Corners: On floor exercise there are four points (corners) in which the gymnasts line up and take turns cross tumbling. Corners are also used to distinguish a floor pattern for floor routines

Cross Tumbling: When gymnasts begin at the corner of the floor and tumble across diagonally

D

Deduction: Points taken off a gymnast's score for errors. Most deductions are pre-determined, such as a 0.8 deduction for a fall from an apparatus or a 0.1 deduction for stepping out of bounds on the floor exercise as described in the judges Code of Points.

Difficulty Level: Each skills assigned a difficulty level "A" (lowest) to "E" (highest) as determined by the Code of Points

Difficulty score ("A" Score): For elite level gymnastics the degree of difficulty contained in the routine.

Dismount: The way the gymnast leaves an apparatus at the end of a routine.

Dive Roll: The gymnast runs and jumps with both feet and the hands and feet are off of the floor simultaneously before a forward roll

Double Back: A backwards double flipping salto. Can be done in a tuck, pike, open, or layout.

Double Front: A forwards double flipping salto. Can be done in a tuck, pike, open, or layout.

Double Full: A single layout salto with two twists

E

Early States: Mid-season states sometimes offered for compulsory levels

Elements: Skills required in a routine

Elite: The highest level in USAG Gymnastics

Endurance: A muscle's ability to continuously perform without growing tired or losing momentum.

Execution: Form, style and the technique used to complete the skills constitute the level of execution of an exercise. Bent knees, poor toe point and an arched or loosely-held body position are all examples of poor execution

Execution score ("B" Score): A routine starts with a maximum of ten points, with execution errors subtracted during the routine. In Elite the execution score is also called the "B" score and is added to the "A" score

Extension: Extension of a joint is moving toward straightness

F

Fall: A fall can be when a gymnast comes off the apparatus before dismount or falls on the floor. Touching the beam to regain balance or feet touching the floor on bars, even if the gymnast doesn't fall off the bars.

FIG: The International Gymnastics Federation is recognized by the International Olympic Committee and is responsible for the governance of the sport of gymnastics on the international level.

Flexibility: The range of motion through which a body part can move without feeling pain.

Flic-Flac: See Back Handspring.

Flight Skill: A flight skill is any skill where the gymnast becomes completely air born in the move before the hands touch the apparatus.

Flip: Tumbling element that rotates hip overhead about the transverse (horizontal) axis. Also called somersault, a salto or somie.

Flyaway: A dismount from the bars. In a flyaway, the gymnast swings forward, releases, and performs a back flip off of the bar

Forward Roll: Starting upright in a standing position the gymnasts reaches for the floor, tucks their chin and rolls forward on the floor with their upper back (not the head) touching the floor, landing back onto their feet and into a standing position.

Front Handspring: A gymnast runs into a handstand blocks off the floor through their shoulders and lands on two feet

Front Limber: A handstand that falls into a bridge and then stands onto feet pushing thru hips and shoulders in an arch position.

Front Support: A front support is usually done on the bars. The gymnast is upright and on top of the bar supported by straight arms.

Front Tuck: Take off two feet rotates forwards, hip overhead, then lands again on the feet. Also called Front Salto, Front Somersault. Other versions: Front Pike and Front Layout.

Front Walkover: Starting on one leg, the gymnast lunges forward passing through a handstand position in a side split by bringing one foot, then the other over the top into a bridge and standing up on one foot.

Full: A back layout with one full twist in the longitudinal axis

G

Giant: A swing in which the body is fully extended and moving through a 360 degree rotation around the bar.

Glide: This skill can be done in a pike or a straddle position and is a swing on a bar that is too close to the ground to swing with a straight body. This skill often precedes the Kip.

Grips: Grips are the leather straps that gymnasts wear to help keep a better grip on the uneven bars. The purpose of grips is to help maintain a firm grip on the equipment and to help minimize the occurrence of rips.

H

Handspring: Springing off the hands by putting the weight on the arms and using a strong push from the shoulders; can be done either forward or backward

Handstand: Gymnasts reach for the ground, extending one leg to the air following the second foot as their hands contact the floor their feet touch resulting in the body being vertical and upside down. Then they come down into the standing position or into a forward roll.   It is also done in various leg positions such as stag (one leg bent, the other straight legs apart as in a split), double Stag (both knees bent legs apart as in a split)

High Bar: Refers to the top bar on the women's uneven bars.

Hip Circle: A very basic circling skill done on the uneven bars or high bar in which the body circles around the bar with the body touching the bar at the hips and the hands and arms supporting the body. There are both front hip circles (usually done out of a kip) and back hip circles (done out of a cast). Neither of these skills are used in optional competition any more. Back hip circles are a progression of free hips. Both hip circles are currently used as USA Gymnastics Compulsory skills.

Hollow: A body position, where hips are turned under, the butt is tucked in and the chest is rounded forward.

Hurdle: A transition from a run into a tumbling skill resembling a skip. The hurdle can be done from a full-speed run or a power hurdle is from a two-foot stand.

IAIGC: International Association of Independent Gymnastics Clubs

K

Kip: A bar skill designed to move from a glide or hang on the bars to a support position. The skill is uses transfer of momentum and is done by swinging or gliding (to a fully extended position), bringing the toes to the bar, jamming up the leg and pulling with straight arms up to a front support position.

L

Layout Position: Stretched / straight body position

Layout Step-Out: A hand free tumbling skill where the legs are split and the landing is on one foot and then the other.

Leotard: A one piece, fitted garment, usually made of a light stretch fabric that fits closely to the skin to cover a gymnast's body. It allows for complete freedom of movement in order to be able to perform any gymnastics skill. Leotards are worn for classes, practice and competitions.

Level: In USAG levels are 1-10 & Elite, USAIGC levels are Copper, Bronze, Silver, and Gold & Platinum.

Lever: Gymnast starts in a lunge position, then reaches out towards the floor while their back leg simultaneously raises to the ceiling and returns the opposite direction finishing in a lunge position again.

Long Hang Pullover: aka Baby giant. Pullover on the high bar

Longitudinal Axis: Axis along the spin, runs from head to toes. A right or left twisting motion

Lunge: A starting and landing position where the legs are separated on the floor. Front leg is bent and the back leg straight

Low Bar: The bottom uneven bar

Mill Circle: Revolution on the bar in which the legs are astride and the bar between them.

Mobility Scores: The score required to move up to the next level.

N

NAIGC: National Association Of Intercollegiate Gymnastics Clubs

Nationals: Now referred to as World's, USAIGC Annual competition which includes all that qualified at states and athletes from other countries

NCAA: The National Collegiate Athletic Association is a nonprofit association that organizes the athletic programs of colleges and universities in the United States and Canada.

Non-Sanctioned Meet: A competition where the scores cannot be used to qualify for states

Neutral Errors: These deductions are not execution based but are for stepping out of bounds or violating time requirements, as well as attire or podium violations.

O

Olympic order: The international competition order the events are rotated in, decided by the FIG. Olympic order for women is vault, uneven bars, balance beam and floor exercise.

Onodi: Starting from a back hand-spring position the gymnast performs a 1/2 twist onto the hands, ending the skill as a front handspring step out.

Open Position: An open body angle is any straight line that a joint creates during a skill

Optionals: Levels where gymnast routines are created by the coaches and are required to meet certain criteria.

P

Pike Position: Body position where the body is bent forward at the waist with the legs are straight.

Pirouettes: Changing direction / rotating in a handstand

Pointed Toes: Where the toes and foot are pulled downward so that the line from the knee to the tip of the toes is essentially straight and there is no angle in the ankle emphasizing a long straight leg and body line.

Press Handstand: A fundamental strength skill in which the gymnast slowly lifts the legs backward to an inverted position while supported on the hands.

Prone: Body position with the front of the body facing the floor, body straight.

Pull Over: On bars the gymnast pulls the legs up and over the bar while bending the arms and ends in a front support.

Punch: Refers to the gymnast bouncing off of the floor with straight legs, pushing through toes & ankles utilizing the spring floor. Opposed to jumping which involves bending the legs and pushing.

R

Rebound: Refers to the gymnast bouncing off of the floor with straight legs, utilizing the spring floor after a tumbling skill.

Regionals: The country is split up into regions. USAG gymnasts qualify for regionals from state championships. USAIGC gymnasts can attend a regional championship in place of states to qualify for Nationals / Worlds

Release: Letting go of the bar to perform a move before re-grasping it.

Rip: When a gymnast works so hard on the bars tear off a flap of skin from their hand. The injury is like a blister that breaks open on the hands or fingers

Rotation: This is the name for the circular motion around an axis of the body.

Round-off: A skill similar to a cartwheel, but with both feet landing at the same time. It is almost always the beginning skill for all back tumbling passes.

Routine: A combination of skills on an apparatus

Running Tumbling: Tumbling that is performed with a running start and/or involves a punch, cartwheel, round-off, round-off handspring, etc., used to gain momentum as an entry to another skill. Any type of forward momentum/movement prior to execution of the tumbling skill(s) is defined as "running tumbling."

S

Salute: It's not only to show respect, though that's a key reason. The salute also plays a critical communication role between gymnasts and judges. Before a gymnast's routine, the judges indicate that they are ready to watch the performance by having one judge raise an arm or by flipping on a green light. The gymnast must then salute the judges to indicate that he or she is ready to begin. Gymnasts also have to salute at the end of their performance. This signals that the routine is complete

Sanctioned Meet: Competition where the scores can be used to qualify for states

Scale: In ballet or gymnastics, when the leg is raised high (ideally to a 180 degree split) while balancing on the other leg. Typically done on beam and may be done to the front, back or side and with the upper body lowered slightly.

Scratch: When a gymnast does not compete in an event or at a meet.

Scrunchie: Fabric-covered elastic hair tie. Many leotards come with a matching scrunchie.

Sequence: Two or more skills which are performed together

Set: The initiation of most aerial/salto skills. For example; a set for a back tuck is when the athlete leaves the floor stretching their arms towards the ceiling, lifting their chest, and spotting the wall in front of them. A set is often counterintuitive and therefore takes focus and determination to maximize its effectiveness.

Shoot Over / Over shoot: A release move from the high bar to the low bar. It starts on the on high bar facing low bar. The gymnast swings up and over the low bar with a half turn to a catch of the low bar.

Shushunova: The gymnast jumps up in straddle position (or other jump position), and rotates her body forward to become parallel to the mat or beam. She then falls to lie face down.

Side Somi: A tuck in the sideways position. Can be performed, running, or from a cartwheel or round-off entry.

Sole circle: Revolution on high bar or the uneven bars in which the feet, as well as the hands, remain on the bar.

Somersault/Salto: An acrobatic skill where the body makes a complete aerial turn (360 degrees) in the transversal axis. Can be done forward, backward and sideward.

Specialist: A gymnast that competes selected events as opposed to competing All Around. A gymnast that competes only pommel horse would be referred to as a pommel horse specialist. This often, but not always, allows for a higher degree of competency on the specialized event.

Split: body position where the legs are extended apart as far as possible in opposite directions. Splits are designated as side splits (right/left) or straddle splits.

Spot: 1) A coach's assistance in a gymnast's attempt to execute a gymnastics skill. 2) The gymnast searches for a point on the opposite wall or floor before initiating a turn or rotation in order to help orientation

Springboard: The takeoff board used for vaulting and performing mounts on other events

Standing Tumbling: A tumbling skill performed from a standing position without any previous forward or backward momentum.

Start Value: The score the gymnasts begin with before deductions in optional levels

States: Championship held in each State is commonly referred to as "States" Gymnasts must qualify for States during the season. Lower levels USAG 1-3 depends on the state and sometimes have "Team Cups"

Step Out: On tumbling skills, this means that an athlete lands on one foot and then the other as opposed to landing on both feet simultaneously

Stick: Slang term used for when a gymnast lands with no movement of the feet.

Straddle: In a straddle an athlete's legs are separated to the side with neither leg being forward or backward of the other. Hips are turned out with knees facing the ceiling.

T

Tap Swing: A proper Tap Swing requires attention to body position: The body, in its rear-most position on the bar, swings forward in a hollow position. At the bottom of the swing, the feet remain still, and the upper body continues to swing, creating an Arch. Quickly, the body returns to a hollow position, and the swing travels forward and upward. The quick Hollow-Arch-Hollow motion is the Tap.

Tight: A tight body position that is not simply straight or extended. The muscles involved in the extension are squeezed and controlled. Positions are held rigid so that different parts of the body can move together. Much of an athlete's strength training is to enable "tightness".

Timer: A drill that simulates the feel of a skill, or the set for a skill without the risk of completing the skill

TOPS: Talent Opportunity Program is an USAG talent search and educational program for female gymnasts ages 7-10 and their coaches.

Transverse Axis: Axis at the waist. Flips that are hips over head

Tsuk: (Tsukahara) A vault where the gymnast jumps off the springboard and performs a quarter turn onto the horse (also known as ½ on) then pushes off her hands and does a back flip

Tuck: A position in which the knees and hips are bent and drawn into the chest; the body is folded at the waist.

Tumbling Pass: A series of connected tumbling elements.

Turnout: In gymnastics and ballet, a rotation of the leg which comes from the hips, causing the knee and foot to turn outward, away from the center of the body. This allows for greater extension of the leg, especially when raising it to the side and rear and for better balance when performing dance skills and on beam. This characteristic most distinguishes ballet from other forms of dance. It refers to the outward rotation of the legs in the hip socket, so that if one were to look at the feet in first position (heel to heel), they would appear to make a straight line.

Twist: A skill where there is rotation along the longitudinal axis so the body is both twisting and flipping.

U

Under grip / Under grasp: Holding a bar with the palms towards face.

Under wrap: Foam that is placed under athletic tape to help protect skin from tape chafing.

USAG: USA Gymnastics is the National Governing Body for the sport of gymnastics in the United States

USAIGC: United States Association of Independent Gymnastics Clubs

V
Valdez: Back walkover starting from a position sitting on the floor

W
Walkover: The gymnast starts from standing on one foot through a handstand position, through inverted split and one footed bridge positions to return to stand. Can be done forward and backward.

Whip Back: Back handspring with no hands. Not to be confused with a back layout which has a straight body position, or a back tuck which is in a closed body position

Wolf Jump: Jump where one leg is extended forward and straight and the other is bent in knee to chest

Worlds: World Championship, previously called Nationals, USAIGC Annual competition which includes all that qualified at states and athletes from other countries

X

Xcel: USAG Program designed to offer a more broad-based, affordable competitive experience outside the traditional Jr. Olympic Program

Y

Yurchenko Vault: Round-off entry onto the vault springboard, Back handspring onto the vaulting table and salto off of the vaulting table. The gymnast may twist on the way off.

These worksheets are for you to gather information into one place. Most if not all these questions should be answered in your gyms policy handout / booklet. Make sure you read your gym's policy handout cover to cover! If they don't have one this is some of the basic information you will need. I recommend using a pencil so you can update it as thing change.

Gym General Policies & Information

Billing Payments & Due Dates

Tuition	Tuition Due Date
Meet fees	Late payment fees
Clinics / Other expenses	Coaches Fees

Meet Policies

How do you scratch a meet?

Practice Policies

Practice viewing policy

Attendance policy

Sick-leave policy

Is there a Parent Association or booster club

What do they cover?
Is there membership dues?
How many volunteer hours parents are expected to serve?
How often are team meetings or parent booster club meetings?

Communication

How does your gym communicate information to you?

How do you communicate to the gym?

General Questions
Meet Scratches
Absences

The Mobility Policy

Scheduled days the gym is closed (any holidays or annual shut down)

Differences between summer schedule and school year schedule

Increased hours for the summer?
Change in time of practice?
Required summer camps?
Is there a scheduled break?

Uniform

Do different levels wear different competition leotards?
Are there used leotards / warm-ups available?
How often are team leotards and warm-up styles changed? Does it pay to buy warm-ups to grown into
Are there practice leotards required?

Level Specific Policy & Information

Level
Practice Days/Time
Required number of training hours
Tuition

Estimated Meet / Coaches fees					
# Required meets		Estimated # Local Meets		Estimated # Travel Meets	

Is there a team hairstyle or scrunchie?

Who do you contact last minute for a meet? For example if you're lost, car trouble, sickness etc.

Contacts

My Gym

Name			
Address			
Website			
Phone		Fax	

Head Coach

Name			
Phone		Email	

Level Coach / Other Coaches

Name			
Phone		Email	
Name			
Phone		Email	
Name			
Phone		Email	

Billing

Name			
Phone		Email	

Parent Association

Name			
Phone		Email	
Name			
Phone		Email	

Fellow Team Parents

Parent's Name			
Child's Name			
Home Phone		Email	
Cell Phone		Other	
Parent's Name			
Child's Name			
Home Phone		Email	
Cell Phone		Other	
Parent's Name			
Child's Name			
Home Phone		Email	
Cell Phone		Other	
Parent's Name			
Child's Name			
Home Phone		Email	
Cell Phone		Other	
Parent's Name			
Child's Name			
Home Phone		Email	
Cell Phone		Other	
Parent's Name			
Child's Name			
Home Phone		Email	
Cell Phone		Other	

Parent's Name			
Child's Name			
Home Phone		Email	
Cell Phone		Other	
Parent's Name			
Child's Name			
Home Phone		Email	
Cell Phone		Other	
Parent's Name			
Child's Name			
Home Phone		Email	
Cell Phone		Other	
Parent's Name			
Child's Name			
Home Phone		Email	
Cell Phone		Other	
Parent's Name			
Child's Name			
Home Phone		Email	
Cell Phone		Other	
Parent's Name			
Child's Name			
Home Phone		Email	
Cell Phone		Other	

Sample Scorebook Page. Available on Amazon.com, Barnes and Noble, www.DBAAthletics.com and select bookstores by Deborah Sevilla. Similar books are available for martial arts, competitive dance, softball, baseball and more.

Meet		Date	
Level		Age Div	

Event	Score	Place
Vault		
Bars		
Beam		
Floor		
All Around		

I STUCK MY LANDINGS!

WHOO HOO!   WHOOPS

My Team Did Great Too!   My Team Placed [ ]

Name	Vault	Bars	Beam	Floor	A.A.

I'm so proud! This meet I...	The HIGHLIGHT was...

For the next meet I'm going to work on...

I Feel like I did...	Vault	Bars	Beam	Floor
THE BEST EVER!				
Better than last time				
OK, The same				
Ugh, I'll do better next time				

Photo Op!

Made in the USA
Middletown, DE
18 December 2014